MODERN DAY
PROVERBS

Profound Wisdom. Plain Language.

GOBEN HILL PUBLICATIONS

© 2010 Godzchild, Inc.

Published by Godzchild Publications
a division of Godzchild, Inc.
22 Halleck St., Newark, NJ 07104
www.godzchildproductions.net

Printed in the United States of America 2010— First Edition
Book Cover designed by Patricia Tibere of ThinkDesignz Media

Library of Congress Cataloging-in-Publications Data
Modern Day Proverbs: Simple Language. Profound Wisdom/Lawrence Q. Alexander II. Includes bibliographical references and scriptural references.
ISBN 978-0-9840955-3-7 (pbk.)
1. Alexander II, Lawrence. 2. Christianity 3. Inspiration 4. Religion

2010930898

Unless otherwise indicated, Scripture quotations are from the New Living Translation.

Table of Contents

MODERN DAY PROVERBS
Simple Language. Profound Wisdom.

Foreword

Convicting. Comical. Creative. These are just a few of the many words that come to mind after reading this masterful literary offering. *Modern Day Proverbs* feeds the sheep of today with the poetry of yesterday. *Modern Day Proverbs* saturates the soul with the water of God's word, and purifies the impure with a touch of heaven on earth. *Modern Day Proverbs* is just what the doctor ordered for this time and for this season! Not only is it a collection of wise sayings and profound puns, but it is one of the greatest examples of the way in which Jesus taught his disciples over two thousand years ago.

Today's culture has tempted many Christian authors to sway toward and sink beneath a kind of secular Christianity that conveniently annotates God in a footnote or endnote. But, *Modern Day Proverbs* reminds us that the Word still works. Of this will you be certain when you finish this innovative assortment of illustrations and meditations. Minister Alexander stands against the impulse to overlook God in the name of spiritual self-help'ism, and instead, challenges each Christian reader to revitalize the Scriptures in a manner that might cause the world to ask again and again, "What must I do to be saved?"

In *Modern Day Proverbs*, we are given God's best expression of love and language. We are introduced to an up-to-date snapshot of what it must've been like to be Solomon. Solomon didn't think like his contemporaries; he didn't pray the same old prayers. He didn't write in the same old style. He was an anomaly to say the least—given much

wisdom for a withering nation.

And indeed, to whom much is given, much is forgiven. This mantle and responsibility of truth-telling (and wisdom sharing) is no different for my great friend, Lawrence. In this book, Lawrence will give you wise instruction, picturesque analogies, and scriptural foundation to suit the needs of all people. Not only does he expose us to the struggles of many characters in the Bible, but he also exposes us to his own struggles and contemplations. As well, he does not just provide pictures and words, but he makes them come alive.

Whether you are seeking, curious, experienced, mini, major, middle—this collection of proverbs will move you from one way of seeing God to another. Get started reading! I promise—you will never ever be the same!

Shaun Saunders
Duke Divinity '10
Author of *Seeing God In Everything*

Introduction

2 Their purpose is to teach people wisdom and discipline,
to help them understand the insights of the wise.
3 Their purpose is to teach people to live disciplined and successful lives,
to help them do what is right, just, and fair.
4 These proverbs will give insight to the simple,
knowledge and discernment to the young.
5 Let the wise listen to these proverbs and become even wiser.
Let those with understanding receive guidance
6 by exploring the meaning in these proverbs and parables,
the words of the wise and their riddles.

Proverbs 1:2-6 (NLT)

King Solomon himself, Israel's wisest king, penned the Book of Proverbs in the Old Testament for a mostly illiterate audience. In his infinite wisdom, King Solomon knew that he had to craft God's Word in a way that his audience, who were unable to read, could understand. To that end, he developed "proverbs" or "wise sayings," short phrases that expressed long ideas. By employing proverbs, Solomon gave his audience knowledge for their heads that could fit in their pockets. He could have overwhelmed them with his intellect, but instead he utilized profound simplicity in his ministry. How considerate was Solomon, not to limit the kingdom of God to the fortunate few who could tolerate the onslaught of intellectual arrogance?

There is one thing the modern church is missing today – simplicity. God's people are unable to understand God's Word and God's clergy are unwilling (and some unable) to make the Word plain. The majority of the church is biblically illiterate and the rest biblically disinterested. Could some of this be the laziness of the people? Sure. Could most of this be the inability of the church to plainly place the Word of God on the plates of God's people? I think so. *Modern Day Proverbs* is one author's earnest attempt to make God's Word understandable so that God's people feel a part of God's family, not His fan club.

Furthermore, there are several people who live outside of fellowship with Jesus Christ, not by choice, but by circumstance. We often refer to them as "lost" when in reality, they've been left. We all have a co-worker, family member, or neighbor that we pass everyday, in full knowledge that they're dying spiritually. Some of us even pass them on our way to church or bible study. Here we are as believers, in full relationship with the Physician, and won't share His number with the sick. God help us!

Therefore, whether you are a non-believer curious about Christianity, a believer who desires a teaching tool that will help you understand the Word for yourself, or clergy who wants to make your preaching more effective and memorable, *Modern Day Proverbs* provides aid in two ways:

Introduction

- ➢ **Evangelism** – *Modern Day Proverbs* is your "conversation starter." You can read and learn innovative ways to engage in meaningful dialogue about our Lord and Savior Jesus Christ.
- ➢ **Edification** – you can give the book to someone to read or even better – read it along with them! Together, you can introduce them to Jesus Christ through a 31-chapter walk through God's Word.

Modern Day Proverbs is a devotional, journal, bible study, and sermon series rolled into one. Whether you talk to God every day or have not talked to him a single day; if it is your desire to know God for yourself or introduce Him to someone else then *Modern Day Proverbs* is for you.

Modern Day Proverbs can help you right where you are as we all come to God seeking something different. Regardless of what you are seeking, it is my prayer that you are enlightened and that our Lord is glorified as you take this journey! Blessed reading!!

The storm isn't over just because the rain has stopped.

Stepping Out Too Soon

13 Noah was now 601 years old. On the first day of the new year, ten and a half months after the flood began, the floodwaters had almost dried up from the earth. Noah lifted back the covering of the boat and saw that the surface of the ground was drying.
14 Two more months went by, and at last the earth was dry!
15 Then God said to Noah,
16 "Leave the boat, all of you—you and your wife, and your sons and their wives.

Genesis 8:13-16 (NLT)

Waiting too long has never killed anyone, but stepping out too soon has. If we're going to trust God with the beginning and the end, then we need to trust Him with the middle, too. The attribute here, in one word, is obedience. Disobedience has killed more people than cancer. Disobedience has fired more people than two-hour lunch breaks. Disobedience has put more people in debt than the credit card industry. Disobedience has ruined more relationships than bad advice. Our disobedience, not God's impotence, is the chief reason we suffer the way we do. There are certain situations in our lives that we have asked God to save us from, He's saved us from them, and then we've ended up RIGHT

BACK where we started. Been there? Well, let's glean some lessons from this passage together as we consider the topic, "Stepping Out Too Soon."

The story of Noah and God's ark receives the attention but the lesson of Noah's obedience and God's instruction steals the show. The story of "The Great Flood" is legendarily referred to throughout both religious and secular circles. When recalling the story, most people credit the ark for saving Noah and his two-by-two band of God's creation, but it was God's Word not God's wood that buffeted Noah and his family from the ravaging waters of the flood.

> "...love for God is manifested through obedience to God. God is not interested in our lip service; He's interested in our life service."

The story of Noah and the Ark is truly a biblical love letter between one man's faith and God's instruction. The bible tells us that Noah was, "a righteous man, the only blameless person living on earth at the time, and he walked in close fellowship with God." Noah had a deep relationship with God. Important to note here: Noah's love for God was evidenced through his obedience to God. I need someone to get that in their spirit – love for God is manifested through obedience to God. God is not interested in our lip service; He's interested in our life service.

If any one of us claims to love God but not do what God says, we are liars. Hear the voice of Jesus in Luke 6:46(New Living Translation),

"So why do you keep calling me 'Lord, Lord!' when you don't do what I say?" Our Lord is actually offended when we call Him one name and treat Him like another. Merriam-Webster defines the word "Lord" as, "one having power and authority over others." When we refer to God as "Lord", we are implying that we are subject to His authority and obedient to His Word. To be disobedient and impatient, then, would utterly disgrace the Lord we claim to love. Calling God "Lord" signifies a relationship with Him and is most readily measured in our obedience to Him. In obedience, Job suffered devastation and did not curse God (Job 1:22). In obedience Jesus suffered the pain of the cross even unto death (Matthew 26:39). Obedience causes us to do what God says, no matter what He says. Disobeying God and then calling Him "Lord" would be like calling your partner "wife" or "husband" and then cheating on them. Noah had a special relationship with God, one we should aspire to. Noah loved God and obeyed God.

The evidence of this relationship is tightly strung through the story of the Ark:

➢ *Noah built the Ark at God's instruction for nearly 100 years with no sign of rain (Subtract Genesis 5:32 from Genesis 7:6).*
> 100 years! God gave Noah instructions that took nearly a century to complete. How long would you wait on God?

➤ *Noah placed his family in the Ark (Genesis 7:13).*

It is one thing to trust God with your life, but a completely other matter to trust God with your family. By faith, Noah placed his wife, his two sons, and their wives in the Ark with him. Do you trust God with your family?

➤ *Noah waited on God's Word, not the world, to step out of the Ark(Gen 8:18).*

Challenge Questions

1. In what areas of your life do you find it most difficult to trust God?

---

2. What consequences have you met as a result of "stepping out too soon?"

---

3. What lessons have you learned?

The Bible approximates that Noah waited for 1 year and 27 days(Subtract Genesis 7:6 from Genesis 8:13-14) after the flood ended to step out of the boat. Noah knew that the God who sent the Ark also sent the flood and He waited on God's Word to leave the Ark.

Noah's trust in God and obedience to God empowered him to wait on God. He waited 100 years for a blueprint, endured a 40-day storm that took 392 days to subside, and waited 2 months after he saw "dry ground" to step out of the boat. Family, the question is clear: How much do you trust God? Your relationship is not measured in the vain dangling of your tongue, but in the upright posture

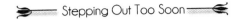

of your faith. Wouldn't it have been a shame for Noah to go through all the trouble of building that ark and saving his family, to lose them all because he stepped off the boat too soon? Remember that Noah's family, future, and ministry depended on his obedience to God. Who's depending on your obedience?

The storm isn't over until God says it's over! Don't go by the water on the ground; go by the God of the ground! Go by the Word, not the world. Family, I encourage you to take inventory of your faith. God can save you from everyone except yourself.

Remember: Waiting too long has never killed anyone,
but stepping out too soon has.

Memory Verse: *Trust in the Lord with all thine heart, and lean not to thine own understanding. In all thy ways acknowledge Him, and He will direct thy path. – Proverbs 3:5-6*

MODERN DAY

PROVERBS

2

You CAN Look Again!

You can start a new chapter in your life, when you and God get on the same page...

You CAN Look Again!

^{1}*Then Jonah prayed unto the LORD his God out of the fish's belly,*
^{2}*And said, I cried by reason of mine affliction unto the LORD, and he heard me;*
out of the belly of hell cried I, and thou heardest my voice.
^{3}*For thou hadst cast me into the deep, in the midst of the seas; and the floods*
compassed me about: all thy billows and thy waves passed over me.
^{4}*Then I said, I am cast out of thy sight; yet I will look again toward thy holy temple.*

Jonah 2:1-4

It's difficult to accept God's love when you've rejected God's Will. Too often, we turned aside from God's way to venture life on our own. For many of us, this prodigal road is paved with painful consequences and regrettable behavior. In this way, we've become our own gods and worship at the altars of stubbornness and self-reliance. Sadly, the price of self-reliance is often too high for us to pay. Thank God we have a Savior, that even after we stray, makes reconciliation possible. Even after you've looked away from God it's good to know that "You CAN Look Again!"

Enter Jonah, the reluctant racist turned prophetic preacher. From the very outset of the book named after him, Jonah can be found running from God. In fact, the first thing Jonah does after God calls him is run. In Jonah 1:2 God says, "Arise, go to Nineveh, that great city, and cry against it; for their wickedness is come up before me." In Jonah 1:3a the Bible says, "But Jonah rose up to flee unto Tarshish from the presence of the LORD..." No sooner than he was called by God was Jonah running from God.

> "So many of us beg God to speak to us or to show us His will, but no sooner than God can reveal it to us, do we start running."

So many of us beg God to speak to us or to show us His will, but no sooner than God can reveal it to us, do we start running. Has this been you? Is there an area in your life right now that finds you running from God? Well if you find yourself like Jonah, doing the "running man" from God, then you should know that a couple of things happen when you run from God:

➤ *You incur the wrath of God when you run –*
   "The Lord hurled a powerful wind over the sea, causing a violent storm that threatened to break the ship apart"- Jonah 1:4 Please don't fall into the fairy tale, fantasizing that God is all soft and cuddly. As surely as it is in God's character to love, it is ALSO in His character to be just. Remember, God wasn't angry at Jonah; He was simply repaying Jonah's disobedience. God in His character must always

reward faith and punish sin. "Yes" makes God smile; "No" makes God frown.

➢ *You endanger others when you run* – *"And since the storm was getting worse all the time, they asked him, "What should we do to you to stop this storm?"- Jonah 1:11* It wasn't simply enough for Jonah to run from God and incur His wrath, but Jonah had the nerve to join company with innocent bystanders. The storm that God stirred up just for Jonah now threatened to create collateral damage for the other men on the ship. My brothers and sisters, know this – when you run from God, you endanger the lives of ALL those around you – friends, family members, loved ones, etc. If you don't love yourself enough to answer God's call, at least consider them.

➢ *You risk your own life when you run* - *"Throw me into the sea," Jonah said, "and it will become calm again. I know that this terrible storm is all my fault." - Jonah 1:12* The only conclusion Jonah could come to, the only sacrifice he surmised that would satisfy God was to cast himself into the stormy sea. Jonah was prepared to commit suicide. Take this seriously family - running from God can drive you out of your mind! The hell unleashed by your disobedience can drive you to the brink of death. Nothing goes right until you serve God – your relationships, your rest, your revenue – NOTHING goes right until you serve God.

Jonah prayed (Jonah 2:1-4) from the depths of his soul, inside the belly of a whale. In verse 2, Jonah actually refers to his aqueous detention center as "hell." It was there that sorrow became his pillow and regret became his blanket. From Jonah's perspective, he was in hell. It was from this penitentiary that Jonah prayed, "I am cast out of thy sight; yet I will look again toward thy holy temple." Despite the destitution around him, Jonah remembered the God within him. Though he once ignored God, he knew that God would never ignore him! Right there, in the rank recognizance of hell, Jonah prayed, "I will look again." You should know that, too. No matter where you are, no matter what you've done, you can pray to God – and guess what – He's listening!

> **Challenge Questions**
>
> *1. In what areas of my life am "I running from God?"*
>
> ---
>
> *2. Who/What is suffering as a result?*
>
> ---
>
> *3. What lessons have you learned?*

Perhaps you've been "there" before or are "here" now. It's been your hand that has slammed the jail bars shut. It's been your infidelity that signed the divorce papers. It's been your sin that has caused your consequence. Only you and God know what you're dealing with, but whatever you're dealing with, I know that God can help. It's got to be awfully difficult to ask God to forgive you again, but it sure is nice to hear God say, "You're forgiven, again!" Won't you "look again" toward God? Know that He's "here" when you're "there."

 You CAN Look Again!

Memory Verse: *Oh, what joy for those whose disobedience is forgiven, whose sin is put out of sight! – Psalm 32:1*

MODERN DAY

PROVERBS

3

Going the Extra Mile

Compassion MUST be followed by action. After you walk a mile in another man's shoes, buy him a new pair!

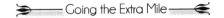
Going the Extra Mile

33"Then a despised Samaritan came along, and when he saw the man, he felt compassion for him.
34Going over to him, the Samaritan soothed his wounds with olive oil and wine and bandaged them. Then he put the man on his own donkey and took him to an inn, where he took care of him.
35The next day he handed the innkeeper two silver coins, telling him, 'Take care of this man. If his bill runs higher than this, I'll pay you the next time I'm here."

Luke 10:33-35

Several of us are civic-minded but too few of us are civically engaged. We are comfortable discussing problems but we are uncomfortable solving them. We're "Monday Morning Quarterbacks" of the spiritual kind. We congregate to talk about everything, talk bad when someone tries to do something, then find ourselves doing what we always do – nothing. So the question comes to us– if you had the opportunity to help your fellow neighbor, what would you do? Cast coins at their feet like a wishing well, pray for them then walk away like an empty altar call or cry sympathetically as you leave them, having done nothing? Our God

gives us specific direction in His Word. Jesus Christ is the Master of Social Work and shows us in this text how to serve by "Going the Extra Mile."

The Parable of the Good Samaritan is commonly looked to as a socio-ethnic religious tale underscoring the importance of caring for our fellowman. While this exegetical insight is true, it only underscores one of several lessons this text teaches. For our purposes, I'd like to highlight one more. Yes, there are many spiritual takeaways from this story (non-prejudicial service, unconditional care for humanity, Christ's salvific personification of indiscriminant sacrifice), but there is one practical lesson that burned in my heart. Jesus not only taught us "who" to serve, He taught us "how" to serve.

"It is an empty faith that puts more emphasis on conformity than service."

Consider our text. In this well known parable, a Jewish man gets robbed on his way to Jericho from Jerusalem by thieves. As the man lay on the side of the road half-dead, he is passed up by two of his own fellow Jews. The first passerby was a Jewish rabbi, whose very calling it was to serve, evaded the man in distress, as he believed the man to be dead (touching the dead was against Jewish Law). The second absconder was a temple assistant who, for the same presupposition (that the man was dead), passed him by. Can you imagine that? Religious folk who were unwilling to help someone in need because it was against their beliefs!

It is an empty faith that puts more emphasis on conformity than service. These men in the text, by religious practice, would have prayed for the man, but would not have touched him. In other words, they would have had compassion but taken no action.

Our text takes a theological turn when Jesus tells us that a Samaritan passes by and does what the good religious folk would not – he helped him! The text states in verse 33, *"Then a despised Samaritan came along, and when he saw the man, he felt compassion for him. Going over to him…"* Remember the social and religious implications of this gesture. The Jews and the Samaritans are sworn enemies; Jews ordinarily have nothing to do with Samaritans. They believe that Samaritans are "heathen" people and allow them no part in their ministry. Wouldn't it then seem like an interesting turn of fate, that the very people they hated, turned out to be the very people they needed? Family, be careful how you treat people – the feet you step on today may belong to the person you need tomorrow! You don't have to love someone to need them, and you certainly don't have to love someone to help them.

Look at how Jesus details the Samaritan's service:

➢ *He healed his wounds - Going over to him, the Samaritan soothed his wounds with olive oil and wine and bandaged them – Luke 10:34a.* The Samaritan could have stopped here; after all, this *is* his enemy. He saw the man in need and helped him with his problem. He didn't owe him any more than that. He gave the poor man a dollar. He bought the hungry woman a sandwich. He sent in his donation to the charity. Wasn't that enough?

Challenge Questions

1. Do I make an effort to help ALL of God's people?

---

2. When I do lend a helping hand, do I put forth my best effort?

---

3. How can I do more to serve my neighbors like Christ served me?

➤ *He carried him to safety - Then he put the man on his own donkey and took him to an inn, where he took care of him – Luke 10:34b.* Even after the Samaritan bandaged the man's wounds, he carried him on his own donkey to an inn. Why you may ask? The answer is because people can't heal in the same place they get hurt. The road between Jerusalem and Jericho was known widely as the path the religious upper class strode to worship. Bandits littered this road at the high times of worship to injure and to rob. This road was not safe for the Jewish man. If the Samaritan merely bandaged his wounds, he would only be delaying a worse fate. Many of us do this – putting band aids on our problems. We band-aid when we should stitch. Pray when we should organize. Donate when we should participate. God requires us to do more than donate; He wants us to participate. Jesus

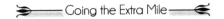

details the aid the Jewish man received for a reason – compassion must be followed by action! The Samaritan's service began with the bandaging, not ended. There's more to our service than "band-aiding."

> *He charged the man's bill to his personal account - The next day he handed the innkeeper two silver coins, telling him, 'Take care of this man. If his bill runs higher than this, I'll pay you the next time I'm here.* This stands out to me as the most profound portion of the Samaritan's service. He not only heals the man's wounds, carries him to safety, but also charges the man's stay in the hotel to his account. Now that's service! Can you see yourself picking up a destitute person, driving them in your car to a hotel, and then pulling out your credit card to charge their stay? It seems ludicrous, doesn't it? Well, before you laugh too hard, remember - this is exactly what Jesus did for us! Wasn't it Jesus that bandaged our wounds of sin, carried them on the cross to Golgotha, and paid the Father with His life so that we may rest in the hotel of eternal life? Jesus went the extra mile for us; certainly we can go a few feet for Him.

There is a mandate on the children of God to serve humanity as Christ did. Compassion alone is not enough. Compassion must be followed by action. We must not only care like Christ cared, we must serve like Christ served.

Memory Verse: *"And the King will say, 'I tell you the truth, when you did it to one of the least of these my brothers and sisters, you were doing it to me!'* *– Matthew 25:40*

MODERN DAY

PROVERBS

4

A Time To Kill

I t's better to live having let go, then to die having held on.

A Time to Kill

1 For everything there is a season, a time for every activity under heaven.
2 A time to be born and a time to die. A time to plant and a time to harvest.
3 A time to kill and a time to heal. A time to tear down and a time to build up.

Ecclesiastes 3:1-3

In life, there are some things you can trust to die on their own, but there are just some things you've got to kill. For instance, you can wait for a light bulb to die before you change it, but you've got to kill a roach the moment you see it. You can wait for a flower to die before you replant your garden, but you've got to kill a weed before it chokes off your plants. Yes, you can wait for some things to die, but there are some things you've just got to kill. You can't wait for the sin-sick cycle of dysfunction, disappointment, and despair to die in your life; you've got to kill it. If I may, let me assure you that this season in your life is "A Time to Kill."

King Solomon is believed to be the author of Ecclesiastes 3. Without objection, Solomon is regarded as the wisest king in all of Israel. His riches and wisdom have never been rivaled. Solomon had more than 1,000 wives, abundant wealth, and fame to boot. As irony would have it,

Solomon penned this book as a eulogy to his rock star status, having truly recognized God's will and the source of true wisdom. Wisdom is not found in the vulgar vigor of one's youth, but in the contemplative consideration of one's maturity. Solomon looked back over the pages of his life and wrote this retrospective, reporting the error of his ways and the righteousness of God.

"...some things in your life need to die, and you need to kill them!"

In our passage, we find Solomon flipping the pages of his life's calendar. In verse 1 Solomon says, "For everything there is a season, a time for every activity under heaven." Very simply, Solomon suggests that nothing lasts forever. Solomon contemplates life as a compilation of "seasons" - cyclical, normal, and necessary variations of God's will in our lives. Life, then, is a series of "seasons" that change, not a static organization of routines that stay the same. Life has seasons, therefore life changes. Solomon devotes the first 8 verses of this chapter describing different types of seasons, but the one that gripped me is found in verse 3, "A time to kill and a time to heal." Of all the seasons, of all the things for a child of God to consider, why on earth would God permit Solomon to tell us that there is "a time to kill"?

Well family, the fact is – some things need to die! The truth may be bitter but it's true nonetheless – some things in your life need to die,

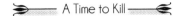
and you need to kill them!

For instance:

> - An unhealthy relationship that robs you of your smile – kill it!
> - A secret addiction that shames you into submission – kill it!
> - An excuse that holds you back from your destiny – kill it!
> - A fear that chases you back into the shadows of suffering – kill it!
> - A relationship with an ungrateful child that refuses to grow up – kill it!
> - A relationship with a stubborn parent who refuses to confess their sins – kill it!
> - A lifestyle that makes you question your answers after you've answered your questions – kill it!

Challenge Questions

1. What am I allowing to live in my life that needs to die?

---

2. Why am I afraid to kill it?

---

3. Is it better for me to live without it or die with it?

Family, there are just some things that will not die on their own. You must find the faith in God to kill the ill that plagues you. "How do I kill it?" you may ask. "Have you tried Jesus?" would be my answer. At Calvary, God did the one thing we were unable to do with our sins—He killed them. His Son became the face of our disgrace to grant us a place in

the kingdom. Thank God on the third day, He raised only Jesus from the tomb; your sins are still safely buried. They will NEVER come back to haunt you again. "How do I kill the sin?" isn't the question; "Who kills the sin" is. Might I suggest Jesus?

You know, the most interesting season follows "A time to kill" in verse 3 – "A time to heal." After you kill the sin in your life, you heal. Just the way that spring follows winter, the once bare trees spring with new life, colorfully and wonderfully. So too will your life spring with the colorful foliage of faith if your root is in Christ Jesus. Wouldn't today be a great day for the seasons to change?

Memory Verse: *No, dear brothers and sisters, I have not achieved it, but I focus on this one thing: Forgetting the past and looking forward to what lies ahead - Phillipians 3:13*

MODERN DAY

PROVERBS

5

The Ultimate Gym Partner

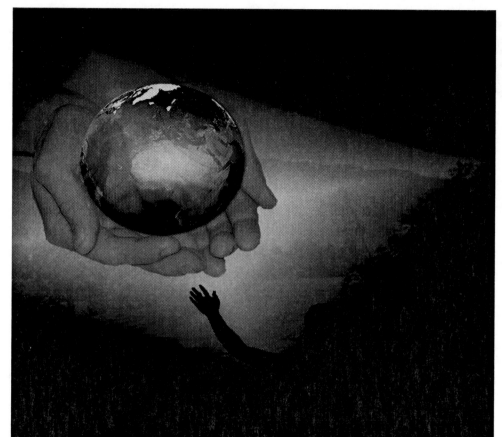

G od didn't take the WHOLE world in His hands for you to carry it on your shoulders. He's a load BEARER, not a load SHARER.

The Ultimate Gym Partner

28 Then Jesus said, "Come to me, all of you who are weary and carry heavy burdens, and I will give you rest.
29 Take my yoke upon you. Let me teach you, because I am humble and gentle at heart, and you will find rest for your souls.
30 For my yoke is easy to bear, and the burden I give you is light."

Matthew 11:28-30

I remember the best gym partner I ever had. Whenever I would get to a difficult place in my routine and the weight would get too heavy for me, he would be right there to "spot" me. I remember one time doing the bench press. I had about 315lbs pounds on the bar, in an attempt to max out after my regular set. My muscles were just fatigued to the limit, and the weight seemed heavier than ever before. I tried with all my might to lift the bar off of my chest, but to no avail. I was afraid – my strength was gone and I could not help myself. I panicked! Right at that moment, my "spotter" was there and he lifted the weight off my chest before it crushed me. Thank God for my "spotter"; he helped me lift a weight that became to much for me to lift.

Family, Jesus Christ does the same for us in the weight room of

life. Jesus is our "spotter" and He keeps the heavy weights of life from crushing us. Indeed, Jesus is "The Ultimate Gym Partner."

Here in our text we find Jesus making us an offer we can't refuse. He calls out to us, "Come to me, all of you who are weary and carry heavy burdens, and I will give you rest." Jesus is making an appeal to a weary people, people who have been accustomed to carrying life's burdens on their own. Have you been there? We often feel like if "we don't do it, it won't get done" so we exhaust ourselves unhealthily. Much like lifting without a spotter, we are forced to lift life's burdens alone. For too long we've been the mother and the father, the father and the mother, the child and the parent, the CEO and the secretary – we've worn all these hats

"...Jesus is prepared to trade our burdens for His peace. God has made relief the repayment for restlessness."

whether they've fit us or not. It is a wearisome and worrisome state to feel overburdened and under supported. Jesus speaks to us to assure us that help is available.

Our Lord declares in His Word, *"Take my yoke upon you. Let me teach you, because I am humble and gentle at heart, and you will find rest for your souls."* In essence, Jesus is prepared to trade our burdens for His peace. God has made relief the repayment for restlessness. The Only Begotten of God is willing to give us comfort in exchange for our discontent. *Where do I sign Lord?!* God our Father loves us so much that He sent His Son to carry a load He didn't create. God sent Jesus to "spot" us with the heavy lifting of life. Matthew 11:28-30 gives us 3 instructions on how to make this peace possible:

> *Come to Jesus* – *"Come to me, all of you who are weary and carry heavy burdens."* There is no way to complain about not getting help if you don't ask for it. The Bible tells us in James 4:8, *Draw nigh to God, and he will draw nigh to you.* The word "nigh" means close: the word "close" means "close". Get close to God and He can heal every hurt you've ever had. Remember, in order for an ambulance to come, you've still got to dial "911."

Challenge Questions

1. What heavy burdens are you carrying?

---

2. What impact is the "heavy lifting" having on your life?

---

3. What good reason do you have not to give your problems to Jesus?

> *Accept Jesus' Way* – *"Take my yoke upon you."* What Jesus refers to here when He says *"my yoke"* is not a physical weight hung from your neck, but rather a way of life that hangs from your heart. Your lifestyle is directly connected to your life stress. Accepting Christ's *"yoke"* means accepting a lifestyle that results in peace. God's blessings are not

accessed by drive thru window; you must come inside His will to receive His peace.

➢ *Learn from Jesus - "Let me teach you, because I am humble and gentle at heart, and you will find rest for your souls."* Jesus' very nature is peaceful. Who but Jesus could endure the indignation of men, the alienation of family, the abandonment of friends and still ask God to *"forgive them, they know not what they do?"* If you're truly going to live for God, your Teacher must be Jesus Christ. You must learn His way in order to do His will. Notice in our text that Jesus is not divinely demanding but patiently appealing, *"Let me teach you.."* Won't you allow Jesus to teach you a new way? Your relief in God is connected to your belief in God. Will you be His student?

➢ *Family, there's no way to get better if you don't do better-*God didn't take the whole world into His hands for you to carry it on your shoulders. The cross is His; the crown is yours. Jesus took a cross on His back so you could take the chip off your shoulder. Isn't today a good day to retire from the restless job of self-reliance? *Remember: The only question God can't answer is the one you don't ask Him!*

Memory Verse: *No, dear brothers and sisters, I have not achieved it, but I focus on this one thing: Forgetting the past and looking forward to what lies ahead - Phillipians 3:13*

MODERN DAY

PROVERBS

6

The House Faith Built

Faith won't keep the rain off your roof, but it can keep the water out of your house...

The House Faith Built

47I will show you what it's like when someone comes to me, listens to my teaching, and then follows it.

48It is like a person building a house who digs deep and lays the foundation on solid rock. When the floodwaters rise and break against that house, it stands firm because it is well built.

49But anyone who hears and doesn't obey is like a person who builds a house without a foundation. When the floods sweep down against that house, it will collapse into a heap of ruins."

Luke 6:47-49

I remember my pastor teaching this lesson in Bible study one night a few years ago. Jesus describes a man with faith as a person, *"building a house who digs deep and lays the foundation on solid rock"* and conversely a man without faith as, *"a person who builds a house without a foundation."* My pastor set the scene of this parable then proposed a question that perplexes me to this very moment. My pastor asked, "What do these two houses have in common?"

It threw me for a loop. "These two houses are nothing alike," I thought. One house was built by a wise man and the other by a fool. One house was built solidly on a rock, and the other neglectfully without a foundation. From my perspective, these two scenarios were like day and night. Suddenly, from the back of the classroom, my uncle proudly cleared his throat, signaling to our pastor that he had an answer to the question. In a confident voice, my uncle shouted, "It rained on both houses!" For some reason, that answer calmed me and disturbed me. Praise God for faith and wise building but why does the rain still have to fall? It seemed unfair to me. There seemed to be no reward to a person's faithfulness. No matter how faithfully you build your home, the rain is going to fall anyway. So then, what's the point in building your life God's way? I'm glad you asked! Faith won't keep the rain off your roof, but it will keep the water out of your house! Please let me talk to you from the subject, "The House that Faith Built."

"If you're going to be faithful enough to get into the ring, then you also need to be prepared to fight."

Jesus didn't teach this parable to protect us from life's storms; He taught it to prepare us for them. Jesus teaches a lesson in faith and demonstrates a lesson in fortitude. He teaches through both the text and the context. Through the text He teaches us to build our homes on a solid foundation; through the context He teaches us that the foundation will be tested. Jesus led with a lesson in faith then followed with a lesson in fortitude. Faith and fortitude go together. If you're going to be faithful enough to get into the ring, then you also need to be prepared to fight. Too many of us are taken by surprise when the oppositional winds of life blow. God doesn't build anything He doesn't test. You wouldn't make a chair you didn't plan on sitting in, would you?

Challenge Questions

1. Do I expect God to shelter me from life or protect me through life?

2. What "storms" has God protected me from?

3. How should my attitude change when I'm facing my next "storm?"

You must always remember: the will of God does not exist in the absence of the suffering of God. We are not immune from the trials of life. God has not promised a life without pain or problems.

Nowhere in the Bible are we promised a lifetime pass from problematic predicaments. The Bible reminds us in Matthew 5:45 that, *"He maketh his sun to rise on the evil and on the good, and sendeth rain on the just and on the unjust."* Suffering is a cup that we're unable to remove from our cabinets.

So what then is the purpose of serving God if He doesn't keep the rain from falling in our lives? Again, I'm glad you asked. The answer is, Everything!

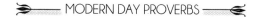
Consider our text again. The foolish man's house was utterly destroyed by the storm, while the wise man's house stood tall. God didn't give him a forbearance from the storm; He gave him fortitude against it! Stop asking God to protect you from the rain; ask Him to protect you in the rain.

The next time you're in the "rain", remember that you could be the man with no foundation!

Memory Verse: *In every thing give thanks: for this is the will of God in Christ Jesus concerning you. – 1 Thessalonians 5:18*

MODERN DAY

PROVERBS

7

A Time to Grow

Take your time with love. Remember, you're trying to make a portrait not a Polaroid.

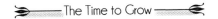

The Time to Grow

Love is patient and kind.

22 Then the Lord God made a woman from the rib, and he brought her to the man.
23 "At last!" the man exclaimed. "This one is bone from my bone, and flesh from my flesh! She will be called 'woman,' because she was taken from 'man.'"

1 Corinthians 13:4; Genesis 2:22-23

What makes a flower grow? Is it the sunlight, with its luminous bath of sunrays and warm kisses? Perhaps it's water, with its aqueous relief from dryness and thirst. I am not convinced that either is chiefly required. Too much sunlight burns the leafy green foliage of flower to a charred, withering brown. Too much water drowns the blooming pupil, depriving it of much needed oxygen. What then makes a flower grow? If it isn't sunlight or water, what is it? I'm glad you asked. In my humble opinion, nothing encourages growth better than time.

Time allows people and things to grow on their terms, not ours. Time allows people and things to grow as God wills them to, not as we desire to. Time permits people and things to develop in the spacious pastures of freedom, not in the deforming confines of our expectations. Yes, time is the chief element required in growth. Time is the most fertile of soil, the most refreshing of water, and the most soothing of winds. People, much like flowers, need time to grow. In case you're standing in the garden of your life right now and have a flower that could use some watering, let me tell you about "The Time to Grow."

Time is the most fertile soil, the most refreshing of water, and the most soothing of wings.

Our twin texts teach us both doctrinally and homiletically. The passage in 1 Corinthians teaches us through God's lesson plan; the passage in Genesis teaches us through God's story book. Whether in God's classroom or God's garden, I do believe that there is a fertile lesson awaiting us.

The 13th chapter of 1 Corinthians is the most quoted chapter at Christian weddings across the world. The chapter underscores the importance of love as demonstrated by its attributes. Much like a tree produces fruit, the text reveals the "fruit" that should develop from our "love trees." In rereading the text, I was arrested by one of the "fruit" described in verse 4: "Love is patient." Of all the things "love is," this one was the most difficult for me. I don't know about you, but I wasn't blessed with a deep wellspring of patience. I am an A-type personality in every sense of the classification. I am scheduled, I am busy, I manage multiple responsibilities, and I want results, now. While this makes me great in a board room, it did nothing for me in my living room. I became argumentative when I should have been understanding, disagreeable when I should have been solution-oriented, and frustrated when I should have been comforting. I failed to give my flower her most important nutrient – time. If you've ever been there, you may have said, "If you can't get it together, then it's not going to work" or "I don't have time for this!" Be careful: someone else will have the time you don't. There's nothing worse than someone "getting it together" the second after the minute you leave.

I often use the second text (Genesis 2:22-23) in pre-marital counseling and wedding ceremonies. The Bible describes what is, effectually, Adam and Eve's first date. God created Adam, gave him a job, a world, and a home – seemingly everything a man could want. As God journeyed on He looked again on Adam is Genesis 2:18 and said, *"It is not good for the man to be alone. I will make a helper who is just right for him."* Why did God create Eve when Adam already had so much? He created Eve because there was one thing Adam didn't have; a companion. None of us makes it through life alone, nor do we want to. Adam's life was productive but it was not yet enjoyable.

God then performed the Bible's first surgery and placed Adam into a deep sleep, removed one of his ribs, and created Eve. So gorgeous was Eve's glow, that at first sight, Adam exclaimed, "*At last!*" Apparently, God wasn't the only one who knew Adam was lonely. In our relationships, we are sometimes tempted to hit the kill switch and end the union. Be careful, you could well be aborting the very thing God has birthed in your life. If you believe that God gave you your mate, then trust that God can fix them too. The problem may not be your partner; it may be the way you see your partner. If you find that you've lost your way, consider Adam's first glance at Eve: "*At Last! This one is bone from my bone, and flesh from my flesh!*" Not only was Eve created for him; she was created from him. Before you leave your Eve, consider that she is meant to be a part of you; not apart from you.

Challenge Questions

1. Am I demanding that my partner grow or allowing them to grow?

---

2. Am I holding my partner to God's expectations or my expectations?

---

3. Am I frustrated because they won't change or because I won't leave?

Why should I give my partner the time to grow? Simple - because you won't know unless they grow. You won't know the kind of wife she can be, the kind of husband he can be, the mother, the father, the pastor, the CEO – you'll never know unless they grow.

The Time to Grow

Know that the question isn't whether or not they'll get there; the question is will you be there when they do?

Memory Verse: *Love never fails – 1 Corinthians 13:8*

MODERN DAY

PROVERBS

8

Filling in the Blank

Being a Christian isn't you checking off a box for God; it's Jesus filling in a blank for you.

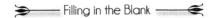
Filling in the Blank

13 When Jesus came to the region of Caesarea Philippi, he asked his disciples, "Who do people say that the Son of Man is?"
14 "Well," they replied, "some say John the Baptist, some say Elijah, and others say Jeremiah or one of the other prophets."
15 Then he asked them, "But who do you say I am?"
16 Simon Peter answered, "You are the Messiah, the Son of the living God."

Matthew 16:13-16

Do you want to know the truth about religion? It's not about affiliation or denomination; it's about proclamation. God doesn't love mega churches more than store front churches or wise old Christians more than new young Christians. God does not discriminate based on your theological preparation or your intellectual reputation. Jesus has made our relationship with the Father as simple as one question – *"Who do you say that I am?"* I'm just grateful that God made salvation an open book exam and only put one question on the test – *"Who do you say that I am?"* To all who seek Christ, salvation will be a simple matter of,"Filling in the Blank."

Our text finds Jesus perusing through society's religious answer sheet concerning His identity. Jesus then administers the exam to His beloved class of disciples. Here Jesus queries, *"Who do people say that I am?"* After a short Google search, the group reports the results - *"Well,"* they replied, *"some say John the Baptist, some say Elijah, and others say Jeremiah or one of the other prophets."* This first grade class responded with a second grade answer. They changed format of Jesus' question. They responded with multiple choices; Jesus wanted them to fill in the blank. Jesus then restated the question – *"Who do YOU say that I am?"*

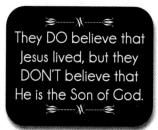

They DO believe that Jesus lived, but they DON'T believe that He is the Son of God.

Let's peel this onion:

➤ *Jesus' question was about religion* – Some people believed that John the Baptist was Jesus, while others believed that He was one of the prophets. The current controversy in religion over Jesus is this same issue. Muslims, Jews, Buddhists, and several of the world's religions debate this same issue today. They *do* believe that Jesus lived, but they don't believe that He is the Son of God. To them, He's just a man – the question Jesus is asking us is - "Who do YOU say that I am?"

➤ *Jesus' question was about relationship* – Jesus didn't pose this question to a group of strangers; He posed it to twelve of His closest friends. Who would know better the true identity of our Lord than the people who were closest to Him? They have sat under His learning tree, eaten from the fruits of His wisdom, and directly witnessed the power of His presence. When our Lord inquires, "Who do YOU say that I am?" He's also asking, "What value does our relationship have?" Listen - Islam, Judaism, Buddhism, Scientology or whatever else may have swayed you – there is nothing and trust me NOTHING like walking in the refreshing cool of Jesus Christ. Jesus not only died for us, but in His life, taught us how to love and to live. After all that Jesus has done for you, who do YOU say that He is?

➤ *Jesus' question was about salvation* – The name you call Jesus will determine what God calls you. When posed the question, Peter declares, "You are the Messiah, the Son of the living God." Peter didn't volley between multiple choices; Peter filled in the blank! In His Word, our Lord declares that, "I am the Way, the Truth, and the Life. No man comes to the Father except through me." Be clear family, our time here on Earth is short. This is not the time to be chasing behind a 5% faith, a Halal holiness, or an Islamic ideal. God is certain about His Son; you need to be, too.

Beloved, the time for games is over. Our Lord through His graciousness has sat back now for over 2000 years while we prostituted

His purpose, cross-dressed His character, and promiscuously played in the bed of pluralism. God is NOT going to accept multiple choices about His singular identity. The prophetic question answered by Peter is posed to you– Who do YOU say that Jesus is?

I'd advise you to find a faith that answers this question. For the true Christian - this is an open book exam! Don't develop a religion; develop a relationship. The relationship will help you find a religion. Just be warned – unless Jesus is His Son, God can never be your Father.

End the masquerade of multiple choices today.

> ### Challenge Questions
>
> *1. Am I afraid of my faith or am I afraid of what others will say about my faith?*
>
> ---
>
> *2. Which need is greater in my life: my need to intellectually understand Jesus or spiritually trust Jesus?*
>
> ---
>
> *3. If I am unsure about Jesus, how can He be certain about me?*

"Who Do YOU Say that I am?" _____ **(Please fill in the blank)**

MODERN DAY

PROVERBS

9

Changing the Channel

L iving in sin is like living in your toilet. It stinks, people dump on you, and no matter how you "flush", the SAME "stuff" keeps happening.

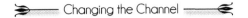

Changing the Channel

Afterward, when Jesus found him in the temple, He said to him, See, you are well! Stop sinning or something worse may happen to you.

John 5:14

I used to like reruns until I became an adult; now they just annoy me. The same shows, same commercials, same plots, and same endings. Reruns have robbed me of my love for classic sitcoms. I used to love "The Honeymooners" when it first came on television, but now that it runs a 24-hour marathon every New Year's Day, it's just not the same. I've gotten to the point where I can recite the script right along with the actors, line for line. The same thing happened to me with the Cosby Show; now I can tell you the episode and season before the opening credits finish rolling. Reruns; it's hard to watch the same thing over and over again. In that way, our lives are like sitcoms – the same shows keep playing over and over again. You know the titles – "Gimme A Break", "Different Strokes", "All My Children", "Divorce Court", "A Different World", and of course my favorite "COPS."

In life, unless you change the channel, you can expect to watch the same old shows over and over again. Might I interest you in "Changing the Channel?"

In our text, Jesus is reunited with the blind man from the infamous "pool at Bethesda." The story is renowned not only because of the healer, but also because of the infirmed. This beleaguered brother had been laying prone in Bethesda for 38 years. The superstitious suspicion was at a certain time when an angel of the Lord stirred the pool up, anyone who was sick could get well. The pool at Bethesda attracted invalids from all over. The pool was a collection point for the blind, the lame, the crooked, and the decrepit. Anyone who was no one could be found at the pool, waiting on their welfare check. This man laid at the pool for 38 years waiting for his "turn." He describes his plight in chapter 5 verse 7, *"Sir, I have nobody when the water is moving to put me into the pool; but while I am trying to come [into it] myself, somebody else steps down ahead of me."* Talk about a bad rerun; this one lasted for 38 years! Day after day, month after month, year after year, this man had to watch the same episode of "Biggest Loser."

Finally, one day, Jesus showed up in the man's life, offering to help him, but because he was so used to making excuses, he became the blockage to his own blessing, *"Sir, I have nobody when the water is moving to put me into the pool; but while I am trying to come [into it] myself, somebody else steps down ahead of me."* What I love here is Jesus' response in verse 8, *"Jesus said to him, Get up! Pick up your bed (sleeping pad) and walk!"* Jesus was unmoved by his excuses. Jesus wasn't interested in what happened in the man's past; He was interested in the man's future. There is a lesson for us in this – God doesn't want to know how you got where you are now, He wants to know where you want to go next. We should shift our focus from the shadows of our past, to the glorious light of our future, sparked by the filament of our present.

The encounter we discover in verse 14 is not chance at all. Jesus had great reason for reuniting with this man and greater reason for including this conversation in the Bible. Jesus had already healed him, but He knew he needed help staying healed. If the man fell back on his old habits, it would only be a matter of time before he was on the breadline at Bethesda again. In verse 14 Jesus says, *"See, you are well! Stop sinning or something worse may happen to you."*

> Stop sinning or something worse may happen to you... the consequences will get worse the second time around.

Jesus knew that the man's lifestyle was connected to his life quality. If the man fell back in sin, he'd fall back on his face. As children of God, we must not only ask God to help us get clean, but also ask Him to help us stay clean. If not, we'll end up a rerun, right back where we started.

Stop sinning or something worse may happen to you. Jesus recommends that we either quit cold turkey or end up dead ducks. Trust that the consequences will get worse the second time around. The first

time is a slap on the wrists; the second time is a night in the slammer. The first time is an accident you can walk away from; the second time finds you unable to walk at all. The first time is a hospital; the second time is a cemetery. God wants us to pump the brakes before we hit the wall.

Not only do we dislike reruns; God doesn't either. When you're ready to "change the channel," God has a new show lined up for you. The show is called "Stairway to Heaven."

Challenge Questions

1. What have the reruns in my life cost me? Time, money, relationships with loved ones, etc?

---

2. What excuse was my favorite? What do I think of it now?

---

3. How many times has God tried to "change the channel" in my life and I insisted on the "station" I was watching?

Memory Verse: *You want what you don't have, so you scheme and kill to get it. You are jealous of what others have, but you can't get it, so you fight and wage war to take it away from them. Yet you don't have what you want because you don't ask God for it. – James 4:2*

MODERN DAY

PROVERBS

10

Watch Your But!

Having a problem isn't a problem; ignoring a problem is.

Watch Your But!

The king of Aram had great admiration for Naaman, the commander of his army, because through him the Lord had given Aram great victories. But though Naaman was a mighty warrior, he suffered from leprosy.

2 Kings 5:1

Yes, it might sound crass, but it's nonetheless true – as a child of God I am directing you to Watch Your But! Yes, we all have a "But." Some of us have big "But's" and some of us have smaller "But's" but we all have "But's." *Watch Your "But"* because your "but" can get you into trouble.

It reminds me of certain and sound advice my dad used to give me before I left the house for school in the morning – "Watch Your But today!" It was a cautionary exclamation, admonishing me to be careful and attentive, because if I wasn't – something bad would happen. If through the course of my day and my travels, I became distracted and lost focus, something bad would happen to my "but." Children of God – "Watch Your But!" because unfortunately, something bad is already happening.

The Bible verse above is one of my favorite Bible stories (2 Kings 5:1-14). In the opening of the passage, we are told of a man named Naaman. Naaman is a great man of military might. He's in high favor with his king, his soldiers revere him, and all the people regard him as a "mighty warrior" BUT Naaman was *dying from leprosy*! Can I spin it this way – Naaman was a big boss on his job, and the CEO let him use the executive washroom and sit at the head chair in the conference room. Naaman was a hoodstar, and everyone knew him when he came on the block. Let's just say that Naaman has "swag" BUT – Naaman was a leper, looking well on the outside but dying on the inside! Naaman had a huge BUT!

Don't mask your inner pain with outer gain.

My brothers, my sisters, we ALL have a "but." I make six figures BUT I can't figure out how to make my marriage work – My body is bangin' BUT my life is banged up – I'm married BUT it's not working out – So many people come to me for help BUT no one's here for me – Feel free to insert your "But" here!

Naaman's "but" highlighted the fact that despite his material possessions and his worldly esteem, Naaman was literally dying on the inside. Sound like anyone you know? So many of us are taught to "fake it till we make it" but all we're making by "faking it" is a mess. Watch Your But! Don't mask your inner pain with outer gain. There is no makeup , no salary, and no degree that can hide your pain from God. You do not have to tell the world your business but make it your business to tell God, who can do the one thing you've been unable to do – Fix Your But!

I challenge you to confess it to God– What's your "But"? For Naaman it was his leprosy, and because of his high profile job, his swanky social status, he attempted to cover his "but" and nearly died. What's your "but"? Is it low self-esteem? Is it depression? Is it a "habit"? Is it an issue you never got help for? Whatever it is, let me assure you – God can fix it! Don't carry this cross another day, let God fix your "But" today.

As hard as it is, deal with your "but" before your "but" deals with you.

Challenge Questions

1. How difficult has it become to mask my issues? Odds are if you're worried about people knowing, they ALREADY know.

---

2. What do I think God will do if I take this issue to Him? I can tell you from experience; He'll fix it!

---

3. What happens if I just put more makeup on my "but?" Naaman almost died trying.

Memory Verse: *Finally, I confessed all my sins to you and stopped trying to hide my guilt. I said to myself, "I will confess my rebellion to the Lord." And you forgave me! – Psalm 32:5*

MODERN DAY

PROVERBS

11

The Faith to Talk When No One's Listening

Personal success cannot be judged in the court of public opinion. Have confidence in the Judge; not the jury.

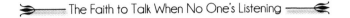

The Faith to Talk When No One's Listening

4 They are a stubborn and hard-hearted people. But I am sending you to say to them, 'This is what the Sovereign Lord says!'

5 And whether they listen or refuse to listen—for remember, they are rebels—at least they will know they have had a prophet among them.

6 "Son of man, do not fear them or their words. Don't be afraid even though their threats surround you like nettles and briers and stinging scorpions. Do not be dismayed by their dark scowls, even though they are rebels.

7 You must give them my messages whether they listen or not. But they won't listen, for they are completely rebellious!

8 Son of man, listen to what I say to you. Do not join them in their rebellion. Open your mouth, and eat what I give you."

Ezekiel 2:4-8

Why should we talk if no one will listen? Why should we teach if no one will learn? Why should we preach if no one will be changed? Why should we love if no one will requite? Fuming with the frustration of a soliloquy masked as dialogue, we retort, *"Well, I might as well be talking to myself!"* Indeed, it is difficult to speak when no one is listening. Why

then does God call us to speak to the spiritually deaf and the rationally resistant? What is the point of appealing to a hard head and a hard heart? I'm so glad you asked. Please let me help you find "the faith to talk when no one's listening."

Our passage eavesdrops on God calling Ezekiel to ministry. God desires a prophet to preach repentance to a hard-hearted Israel. For generations now, the children of Israel have turned their backs on God and become hostile to sound doctrine. God refers to their behavior as "rebellious." In fact, within the four verses of this passage, God uses the word "rebel" in some form, four times! The fact that the Lord is so descriptive of this audience acknowledges the fact that God knew just how difficult a task it was going to be for Ezekiel. Picture this Job Posting – *Wanted: change agent for a rebellious, rambunctious, unrepentant people.* Would you take that gig? I figured not.

"... the places we like the least are where God needs us the most."

Family, the places we like the least are where God needs us the most. You may not like your assignment but God does. You may not understand why you are where you are – the job you're at, the church you're in, or even the family you have. You may not see the purpose in your service, but God does.

There were 3 wayside blessings in store for Ezekiel as a result of answering God's call:

➢ *Confidence through Confrontation* – We don't develop strength through ease. God instructed Ezekiel, "They are a stubborn and hard-hearted people. But I am sending you to say to them, This is what the Sovereign Lord says!" God didn't send the prophets to Israel "because of" their behavior, God sent them "in spite of" their behavior. Know that the "Good News" isn't always "Good" to everyone. Your effectiveness is not measured by your audience's reception. Have confidence in the message, not the recipients. God's approval is not measured in human applause.

➢ *Kingdom success through personal failure* – When we speak, we want the whole world to listen. The fact is that most won't. The Lord cautions Ezekiel, "And whether they listen or refuse to listen—for remember, they are rebels—at least they will know they have had a prophet among them." Know that God isn't interested in the multitude. Consider the parable of the Lost Sheep – the shepherd left 99 "found" sheep in search of 1 who was "lost". God may very well place you in a group of 100 just to convert 1 soul back to Him. Remember, He said in Luke 15:7, "I say unto you, that likewise joy shall be in heaven over one sinner that repenteth, more than over ninety and nine just persons, which need no repentance." Be satisfied

with one and stop mourning over the other ninety-nine.

Challenge Questions

1. Who's your true audience, men or God?

---

2. Who has endowed you with your gift, men or God?

---

3. How do you expect to find His pleasure in their approval?

➢ *Blessings through Obedience* – The password for God to bless is "Yes." When you say "Yes" to God, it "opens the windows of heaven." Remember, Ezekiel's blessings were dependant upon his obedience. He was only appointed a prophet because he said yes to God. The only reason he got the Word from the Lord is because he said yes to God.

Hear the Lord admonish him: "Son of man, listen to what I say to you. Do not join them in their rebellion. Open your mouth, and eat what I give you." The reason Ezekiel got blessed is because he said "yes." No "yes," no bless. In case you want to know why God isn't opening the windows for you, perhaps it's because you're closing the doors to Him. "Yes" is the key that turns the lock!

Family, it's about courage. The courage to talk when no one's listening, write when no one's reading, and sing when no one else is singing.

If God gave you what you have, then He'll also be interested to see what you've got. God is your audience, and He's always listening. Start talking to the world like you're talking to Him. See it as a private conversation gone public.

Memory Verse: *For I know the plans I have for you," says the Lord. "They are plans for good and not for disaster, to give you a future and a hope. – Jeremiah 29:11*

MODERN DAY

PROVERBS

12

The Love That Won't Let You Leave

It's hard to leave God once you've believed God.

The Love That Won't Let You Leave

7 O Lord, you misled me,
and I allowed myself to be misled.
You are stronger than I am,
and you overpowered me.
Now I am mocked every day;
everyone laughs at me.
8 When I speak, the words burst out.
"Violence and destruction!" I shout.
So these messages from the Lord have made me a household joke.
9 But if I say I'll never mention the Lord or speak in his name,
his word burns in my heart like a fire.
It's like a fire in my bones!
I am worn out trying to hold it in!

Jeremiah 20:7-9

It's like an itch you can't scratch, a face you can't forget, a song you can't stop singing. It's irresistible, irreplaceable; you've got to have it. No matter how angry you get or how long you separate, you find yourself back in love again. Most of us associate this amorous espousal with our guy or our girl, but in this meditation, I'm referring to our God. No matter how hard you try, once you've truly accepted Jesus Christ, there is no turning back or running away. Let me put the needle to the vinyl and play you song entitled, "The Love that Won't Let You Leave."

"Jeremiah loves God but dislikes the consequences that serving God entails."

Our text finds the prophet Jeremiah doing his best *"Dear John"* impersonation. Jeremiah has just been arrested and tortured (again) for preaching God's Word(again). Jeremiah loves God but dislikes the consequences that serving God entails. People mock him. He feels foolish. When he wants to speak, God takes control of his mouth. Ever since Jeremiah joined up with God he has been unpopular, imprisoned, and made a public spectacle. Jeremiah was driven to the place that many of us get to – *"What's the point in doing God's will if it causes me this much pain?"* People mock me when I preach. They laugh at me when I dance. They snicker when I sing. They walk out every time I speak up. Ever been there? Sometimes it can feel like we're better off without God.

Can you see the ink on Jeremiah's resignation letter?

> *O Lord, you misled me,*
> *and I allowed myself to be misled.*
> *You are stronger than I am,*
> *and you overpowered me.*
> *Now I am mocked every day;*
> *everyone laughs at me.*
> *When I speak, the words burst out.*
> *"Violence and destruction!" I shout.*
>
> *So these messages from the Lord*
> *have made me a household joke.*

Jeremiah had enough. Momentarily, he was tempted to turn away from God. I'm not sure about you, but I've been there. I've often felt like it would be easier to sin then it would be to serve. I've been resentful about living for God while others get to enjoy the world. Frankly, I've come to points where serving God felt pointless. Like Jeremiah, I've been tempted to walk away from God and back out into the world. *Have you?*

Watch closely here as Jeremiah discloses the reason he burned his resignation letter.

Jeremiah says in verse 19,

> *But if I say I'll never mention the Lord*
> *or speak in his name,*
> *his word burns in my heart like a fire.*
>
> *It's like a fire in my bones!*
> *I am worn out trying to hold it in!*
>
> *I can't do it!*

Family, know that when you give your life to Jesus Christ, He places a permanent brand on your heart. You can't leave God if you wanted to. You know Him now. You love Him now. You serve Him now. There is no turning back! Even if you did venture back into the world, it wouldn't prosper. You'd be the most anointed sinner in the club, the holiest hobo on the corner, and the guiltiest drunk at the bar. The alcohol won't get you drunk, the drugs won't get you high, the

Challenge Questions

1. How far can I get in my life without God in it?

---

2. Who else will love me the way God does?

---

3. What reason do I have for living apart from God?

sex won't satisfy you. You couldn't turn away from God if you wanted to, not because God loves you, but because now – you love Him! It's not God's love for you that will bring you back; it will be your love for Him that won't let you leave.

The word for this moment in your life, is "Continue." Continue to seek God. Continue to serve God. Continue to separate yourself from the things that draw you away from God. On your journey you may be tempted to step back into the world and back into your old ways, but trust me, **Y**our Love Won't Let You Leave. There will be a fire in your bones, a Holy Ghost Hot Flash that calls you back home.

I urge you to know Him if you do not or get reacquainted if you've lost touch.

Memory Verse: *And I am convinced that nothing can ever separate us from God's love. Neither death nor life, neither angels nor demons, neither our fears for today nor our worries about tomorrow—not even the powers of hell can separate us from God's love. – Romans 8:38*

MODERN DAY

PROVERBS

13

God's Problem With Your Solution

JESUS SAVES!

It may be hard to believe in a God you can't see, but it's harder to go to hell for a reason you can't justify.

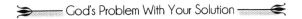

God's Problem With Your Solution

13For "everyone who calls on the name of the Lord will be saved."
14How then will they call on him in whom they have not believed? And how are
they to believe in him of whom they have never heard? And how are they to hear
without someone preaching?
15And how are they to preach unless they are sent?

Romans 10:13-15

"I can build mine without it!" was my response to my wife's suggestion that I use the instruction manual to build our entertainment system. "I can build mine without it!" was the song my stubbornness sang as I pitifully pieced together this wooden structure that was to bear the weight of our television, library, and DVD collection. "I can build mine without it!" was my solution to the problem of building this structure. Well....needless to say, my solution led me to a problem! Soon after I completed the project and threw away my plastic bag of "extra" parts and that "useless" instruction manual, I attempted to put weight on my newly built structure. Family, this was entertainment of a different sort. *"Snap!"* was the song the shelves sang as the books buckled them in the center.

"Crackle, Pop!" cried the choir of avalanching DVD's as the wood splintered under their weight. "Oh man!" fretted I as I frantically formulated how I was going to explain this to my wife. I had attempted to establish a structure without following the directions. There was a problem with my solution.

Don't you know that some of us do the same thing with our faith? Pull up a chair and let me tell you about "God's Problem with Your Solution."

"I can build mine without it!" is the song many of us sing regarding our faith. Many of us believe that we don't need a religion, a church, the Bible, or a preacher to be saved or to have a relationship with Jesus Christ. While I sympathize with those who have been turned off by pimps in the pulpit, money hungry ministries, and perverts parading as preachers, I would not have you ignorant – you need to go to church! While it doesn't have to be your momma or daddy's church or the old people's church on the corner – you need to find a house of God SOMEWHERE! In the same way muscles cannot be developed while sitting on your couch, faith cannot be developed while sitting on your excuses. "I can build mine without it!"

> ⋙--)(--⋘
> *"In the same way muscles cannot be developed while sitting on your couch, faith cannot be developed while sitting on your excuses"*
> ⋙--)(--⋘

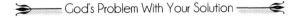

Are you sure about that?

In our text, Paul systematically suggests that building faith necessitates participation in following God's instructions. Using negations as his argument style, he pokes the following holes in our lame "I can build mine without it!" logic. Paul first agrees with the Word of God which states through the prophet Joel, *"Whosoever calls on the name of the Lord shall be saved,"* but then poses these problems with our self-reliant solution:

> *Faith - "How then will they call on him in whom they have not believed?"* Paul first inquires as to our faith. How can you say that God can save you if you don't believe in Him? It's like having a name in your phone without the number, how are you going to make the call? Some people will read and say, "Well I do believe in God," well how does God know? If you "believe in God" then you should "be living in God," otherwise God's house is not your home!

> *The Word of God – "And how are they to believe in him of whom they have never heard?"* There may be many ways to "feel" God, but there's only one true way to know God, and that's through His Word. It is IMPOSSIBLE to establish your faith without the Word of God. The Bible is God's Holy Instruction Manual. It is the Master's Plan for our living, dying, and salvation. How can you call God your Father in Heaven yet not know His Word? No lasting relationship is built on a

superficial sentiment. You can't "kind of, sort of" know God. Jesus would describe this condition as a "house built upon the sand"; when the rain comes it WILL sink!

Challenge Questions

1. I may have had good reason to avoid Jesus to this point. What reason do I have now?

2.How can I expect to deepen my faith in the shallow waters of my mistrust?

3.What excuse can I offer God for not drawing closer to Him?

➤ *Your Instructor – "And how are they to hear without someone preaching?"* Televangelists, E-vangelists, and so forth, can supplement your relationship with God and your knowledge of the Word, but they cannot and must not be your sole source. My only goal is to be a bridge for you to travel over on your way to Jesus Christ and into a house of God. If you are to truly hear from Heaven, you must hear from a man or woman sent by God who preaches the true Word of God.

And to your next question(How do I trust a man or a woman?), Paul already pens the answer in verse 15, *"And how are they to preach unless they are sent?"* God has, is, and always will send those whom He chooses to preach His Word. I know that humans are hard to trust, but believe God through them even if you have a hard time believing in them.

Family, our conclusion and our challenge is this: am I confident in my relationship with God? The hour is drawing near when "weight" will be placed on the faith we have built. Are you sure that you want to build yours on your own? If not, might I suggest a Jesus who died to translate Heaven's Instruction Manual into your language?

Memory Verse: *Trust in the LORD with all thine heart; and lean not unto thine own understanding. In all thy ways acknowledge him, and he shall direct thy paths. – Proverbs 3:5-6*

MODERN DAY

PROVERBS

14

Get Rich and Try Dying!

Not all profits are profitable.

Get Rich and Try Dying!

19 Jesus said, "There was a certain rich man who was splendidly clothed in purple and fine linen and who lived each day in luxury.

20 At his gate lay a poor man named Lazarus who was covered with sores.

21 As Lazarus lay there longing for scraps from the rich man's table, the dogs would come and lick his open sores.

22 "Finally, the poor man died and was carried by the angels to be with Abraham. The rich man also died and was buried,

23 and his soul went to the place of the dead. There, in torment, he saw Abraham in the far distance with Lazarus at his side.

24 "The rich man shouted, 'Father Abraham, have some pity! Send Lazarus over here to dip the tip of his finger in water and cool my tongue. I am in anguish in these flames.'

25 "But Abraham said to him, 'Son, remember that during your lifetime you had everything you wanted, and Lazarus had nothing. So now he is here being comforted, and you are in anguish.

26 And besides, there is a great chasm separating us. No one can cross over to you from here, and no one can cross over to us from there.'

Luke 16:19-26

Be careful about what you value. The capitalistic, democratic, ruggedly individualistic society in which we live has become our new religion. Pulpits promoting prosperity, street corners slinging selfishness, and corporations crooning entrepreneurs have indoctrinated us into a "new" testament with a genesis in greed and a revelation in riches. We worship money and all the things money buys. All of us have been there, and none of us are immune. If we are honest with ourselves, all of us at one point stopped by the church of *Gotta Get Paid* to listen to the sermon, *"Get Rich or Die Tryin."* Well allow Jesus to get a Word in edgewise. Hear His sermonic remix, "Get Rich & Try Dyin'!"

> *"If all we see is all there is, then this is all there ever will be... But aren't you glad there are TWO SIDES to every story?!"*

Jesus loved telling jokes that weren't funny. Here in the 16th chapter of the Gospel according to the physician Luke, Jesus makes a social incision into the hearts of the Pharisees. The Pharisees, the ecclesiastical class of rich cats, prided themselves on their status. They were esteemed religiously as teachers and desired socially as fat cats. From their perspective, they were living "high on the hog." Leave it to Jesus to show them that they were "sleeping in the slop."

Starting at the 19th verse, Jesus hosts a Def Comedy Jam by

spinning a story about a poor man who went to heaven and a rich man who went to hell. Jesus told a "tale of two cities" nestled in His state of righteousness. Jesus described the lots of our two heroes: The rich man, with his fancy purple draws and his fancy feast cuisines and Lazarus, a lesion licking loser. On earth, the rich man prospered while the poor man pandered. The Bible says that the rich man *"lived each day in luxury,"* while poor Lazarus *"lay there longing for scraps from the rich man's table."* One man's success and another man's suffering. The Rich: 1 The Poor: 0. If all we see is all there is, then this is all there ever will be. If the story only has one side, if the game has only one half, if earth is all there is – then the social soliloquy *"Getting Rich or Die Trying"* makes sense. But aren't you glad that there are two sides to every story?! *Feel free to put a praise right there: Glory!!!!*

Jesus turns the page and flips the script on this rag tag tale. In the second half of the story, we now find our rivals' roles reversed just a bit. In eternity, Lazarus is hi-fiving Abraham in heaven and the rich man is sucking spit in hell. Remember, there are two sides to every story. On earth, wealth was a material matter; in eternity, wealth was a spiritual matter. Jesus Christ, the Crown of the Kingdom, came to establish a new world order. From His inception to His resurrection, Jesus redefined what it meant to be "rich."

Several passages point to Christ's social and material reclassification:

➢ *Mark 10:25* – "It is easier for a camel to go through the eye of a needle, than for a rich man to enter into the kingdom of God."

➢ *Mark 8:36* – "For what shall it profit a man, if he shall gain the whole world, and lose his own soul?"

➢ *1 Timothy 6:10* – "For the love of money is the root of all evil: which while some coveted after, they have erred from the faith, and pierced themselves through with many sorrows"

Challenge Questions

1. Where do I place my value?

---

2. How has my value system impacted my decisions?

---

3. Have I used money and loved people or used people and made money?

➢ *Acts 8:18-20* – "When Simon saw that the Spirit was given when the apostles laid their hands on people, he offered them money to buy this power. "Let me have this power, too," he exclaimed, "so that when I lay my hands on people, they will receive the Holy Spirit!" But Peter replied, "May your money be destroyed with you for thinking God's gift can be bought!"

Get Rich and Try Dying!

➢ *Matthew 6:19-20* - "Don't store up treasures here on earth, where moths eat them and rust destroys them, and where thieves break in and steal. Store your treasures in heaven, where moths and rust cannot destroy, and thieves do not break in and steal."

➢ *Luke 6:20* – "And he lifted up his eyes on his disciples, and said, Blessed be ye poor: for yours is the kingdom of God."

Family, not all profits are profitable. You'd be well served to re-evaluate your value system. The rich fat cat in this passage burned in hell with no hope for salvation. Jesus wasn't telling a joke nor am I telling you one. God is real and so is hell; the difference between the two is you. There are those who chase the almighty dollar, but I'd rather chase the Almighty Father. The world can live the dream, "Get Rich or Die Trying" but I'd encourage you to consider what it's like to "Get Rich & Try Dying."

Memory Verse: *"For what shall it profit a man, if he shall gain the whole world, and lose his own soul?" Mark 8:36*

MODERN DAY

PROVERBS

15

A Cup Called Suffering

Faith in God trusts Him with the end,
right from the beginning.

A Cup Called Suffering

42 "Father, if you are willing, please take this cup of suffering away from me. Yet I want your will to be done, not mine."

18 While he was still speaking, another messenger arrived with this news: "Your sons and daughters were feasting in their oldest brother's home.
19 Suddenly, a powerful wind swept in from the wilderness and hit the house on all sides. The house collapsed, and all your children are dead. I am the only one who escaped to tell you."
20 Job stood up and tore his robe in grief. Then he shaved his head and fell to the ground to worship.
21 He said,
"I came naked from my mother's womb,
and I will be naked when I leave.
The Lord gave me what I had,
and the Lord has taken it away.
Praise the name of the Lord!"
22 In all of this, Job did not sin by blaming God.

Luke 22:42; Job 1:18-22

Suffering has a way of promoting prayer. On knees bent by desolation and backs broken by disaster, the world finds themselves praying prostrate on the altar of God's mercy. Human suffering and widespread calamity reign among our chief theological quandaries. How can a loving God permit a parade of pain, suffering, and loss? Natural disasters can preach valuable spiritual lessons. Let me walk you into the kitchen called *Life*, show you to the cabinet called *Kingdom Come*, and pull you out a "Cup called Suffering."

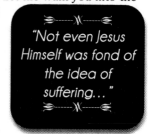

"Not even Jesus Himself was fond of the idea of suffering..."

Rather than exploring a specific text for multiple ideas, I'd like to use multiple texts to promote one specific idea: suffering is a necessary part of life. Contrary to popular opinion, suffering is not derived from God's cruel sense of humor nor from His absent-minded practice of abandonment. God doesn't will suffering for our lives, but He does permit it. Suffering is part of life. No one has ever donned a skin suit called flesh and roamed the dust ball we call Earth and escaped pain-free.

Jesus Christ Himself, the Son of God, suffered the human inevitability called suffering. His prayer, found in Luke 22:42 exposes the fragile humanity of our Savior when He prayed, "Father, if you are willing, please take this cup of suffering away from me." Not even Jesus Himself was fond of the idea of suffering.

A Cup Called Suffering

Our second text comes to us from the book of God's main man, Job. The Bible tells us that Job, "was blameless—a man of complete integrity. He feared God and stayed away from evil." Job was an "A" student in God's classroom, yet the book of Job records how Job lost his children, all his earthly possessions, and nearly his entire mind.

How could it be that God allowed His prize servant Job and His very own Son Jesus to suffer so strongly? I'm glad you asked! God has some specific lessons that only Dr. Suff R. Ing can teach:

➢ *Trust through Dependence* – Pastor Rick Warren once said, "It's only until God is all you have that you recognize that God is all you need." Only the deepest of destitution and destruction can make some of us realize that God is in control. When Jesus prayed in Gethsemane, He was abandoned by all His friends and family. When Job prayed to God, he had lost his children, servants, and property. Suffering tends to be the carpet on which many of us bend our knees in prayer.

It is there and only there that certain Scriptures make sense:

What did David have to endure to declare,

> *"For you are my hiding place; you protect me from trouble." -Psalm 32:7*

What must Paul have gone through to conclude,

> *"I know how to live on almost nothing or with everything. I have learned the secret of living in every situation, whether it is with a full stomach or empty, with plenty or little. For I can do everything through Christ, who gives me strength" (Philippians 4:12-13)*

Destitution gives God a captive audience with you. The reason that God can speak in a "still small voice" is because at these points, you're all ears! Suffering tends to be the spiritual hearing aid most of us need.

➤ *Passionate Prayer* - Suffering is the scent of passionate prayer. It is the aromatic accent of true praise. When you're at your worst, God is at His best. Pray like you've got a problem, then praise like you've got an answer!

Hear Jonah praying from the belly of the whale,
> *"I cried out to the Lord in my great trouble,*
> *and he answered me.*
> *I called to you from the land of the dead,*
> *and Lord, you heard me!*
> *You threw me into the ocean depths,*
> *and I sank down to the heart of the sea.*

The mighty waters engulfed me;
I was buried beneath your wild and stormy waves.
Then I said, 'O Lord, you have driven me from your presence.
Yet I will look once more toward your holy temple.' – Jonah 2:2-4

Challenge Questions

1.It's hard to trust God, but even harder not to. What tempts me to mistrust?

2.How do I see disaster: as a mess or a message?

3.What lessons have God already taught me from the disasters He's brought me through?

Suffering has got to be God's most effective altar call.

➤ *Testimonies through Trials* – the old people used to sing a song, "If I never had a problem, how would I ever know that God could solve them?" God will never put more on us than we can bear. It is on this premise that we should praise God even in the face of disaster.

Hear David reassure us, *"I have been young, and now am old; yet have I not seen the righteous forsaken, nor his seed begging bread."* – Psalm 37:25

Having the faith to persevere is paramount in the lives of God's children. We can't love the God of sun shine but hate the God of rain. Faith in God

trusts Him with the end, right from the beginning.

This is what allows Job to shout,

> *"The Lord gave me what I had, and the Lord has taken it away. Praise the name of the Lord!" (Job 1:21b)*

This is what allowed Jesus to pray through bloody tears,

> *"Yet I want your will to be done, not mine." (Luke 22:42b)*

Family, it's time to bolster our faith. The true child of God examines not the cause behind the calamity but the purpose in front of it. Haiti (and for that matter, the world) is receiving a first class education in God's Sovereignty. "The earth is the Lord's and the fullness thereof" (Psalm 24:1). This world belongs to God and He will turn suffering into salvation right before their eyes. The only question is, "Where will you be when He does?"Cowering in the corner with your fingers crossed or in the front of the class shouting, "I told you so!"

Dr. Suff R. Ing has a boss named Jesus D. Christ!

Memory Verse: *God is our refuge and strength, a very present help in trouble. Therefore will not we fear, though the earth be removed, and though the mountains be carried into the midst of the sea. – Psalm 46:1-2*

MODERN DAY

PROVERBS

16

Jesus' Solution to Welfare

If you give a man a fish he'll eat for a day, but if you teach a man to fish he'll eat for a lifetime.
– Confucious

If you give a man Jesus, he won't need any fish!
– L.Alexander II

Jesus' Solution to Welfare

1 Peter and John went to the Temple one afternoon to take part in the three o'clock prayer service.
2 As they approached the Temple, a man lame from birth was being carried in. Each day he was put beside the Temple gate, the one called the Beautiful Gate, so he could beg from the people going into the Temple.
3 When he saw Peter and John about to enter, he asked them for some money.

4 Peter and John looked at him intently, and Peter said, "Look at us!"
5 The lame man looked at them eagerly, expecting some money.
6 But Peter said, "I don't have any silver or gold for you. But I'll give you what I have. In the name of Jesus Christ the Nazarene, get up and walk!"

Acts 3:1-6

You've heard of the expression, *"If you give a man a fish he'll eat for a day, but if you teach a man to fish he'll eat for a lifetime."* Well, let me offer you yet another way to look at this spiritual and social condition – *"if you give a man Jesus, you won't have to give him any fish!"* The power of our God, given to us in Christ Jesus endows us with the strength we need to stand on our own feet, without "public assistance." Is it alright if I walk you to work and tell you about "Jesus' Solution to Welfare?"

No – I am not referring to welfare our social program; I am referring to welfare, our spiritual practice. The problem for too many of us is that we've had *symbiotic* relationships with God. In other words, we've had a relationship with God "through" someone else. Let me put

"... other people can go to God about you, but no one can go to God for you."

some meat on this skeleton – we won't go to church, but we'll ask someone to pray for us. We won't read the Bible so we depend on others to tell us what's in it. We won't get saved but we'll rely on someone else's relationship with Christ to cover our canker sores. Understand this: other people can go to God about you, but no one can go to God for you. You've got to get high on your own supply!

Consider our text. Here we find Peter and John encountering a local welfare recipient. This lame man sat outside the gate of this temple for nearly 38 years. For 38 years he laid at the gate called Beautiful and begged for money from the local temple worshippers. For 38 years people took pity on him and gave him money. For 38 years his condition stayed the same – LAME. If the truth be told, not only was the man lame but the "church folk" were pretty lame, too. The man was LAME –

crippled, disabled; giving him money was useless. Giving a lame man money is like giving a blind man reading glasses or a deaf man a hearing aide – useless. The problem for too many of us is that we try to give people what they want instead of giving them what they need. This man didn't need money; He needed Jesus!

Family, you've got to see past your wants and understand your needs. Stop asking God to help you with your "lame" situation; invite Jesus into your life so He can change your life! Look at how two men of God helped this lame brother. Peter commanded his attention and then told him, *"I don't have any silver or gold for you. But I'll give you what I have. In the name of Jesus Christ the Nazarene, get up and walk!"*

> ### Challenge Questions
>
> 1. How tired am I of begging and borrowing? How tired are others of me begging and borrowing?
>
> ---
>
> 2. Why can't the same God that blessed everyone else bless me?
>
> ---
>
> 3. How much longer can I be identified by my need and not my name?

Peter denied the man's monetary request but met his spiritual need. The man didn't need gold or silver; He needed something of more value – a relationship with Jesus Christ!

Trust Jesus to be EVERYTHING you need – your Month at the end of the money, your cold night's Furnace, your portable Confessional, your Co-Signor, your resumé, your Career Builder – trust Jesus to be

EVERYTHING you need! It wasn't money that made that lame man walk; it was the power of God through Christ Jesus. Check out the lyrics to Peter's altar call, *"In the name of Jesus Christ the Nazarene, get up and walk!"* All you need to "stand on your feet" is the willingness to get off the mat; Jesus can do the heavy lifting.

The question I challenge you to consider is this: *How long will you lay there? How long will you lay there helpless and dependent? How long will you rely on the kindness of strangers to help you "get by"? How long will you watch others walk by you, pitying you? How long will you be the second-hand recipient of the blessings that you're an heir to? How many altar calls will you come to with the same problem? How long will you be a spiritual welfare recipient?*

If you're tired of the "handouts," why not try Jesus today? He'll teach you to catch more than just fish.

Memory Verse: *Now unto him that is able to do exceeding abundantly above all that we ask or think, according to the power that worketh in us. – Ephesians 3:20*

MODERN DAY

PROVERBS

17

God's Correctional Facility

G od's direction and God's correction go hand in hand; not tongue in cheek.

God's Correctional Facility

7 As you endure this divine discipline, remember that God is treating you as his own children. Who ever heard of a child who is never disciplined by its father?
8 If God doesn't discipline you as he does all of his children, it means that you are illegitimate and are not really his children at all.
9 Since we respected our earthly fathers who disciplined us, shouldn't we submit even more to the discipline of the Father of our spirits, and live forever?
10 For our earthly fathers disciplined us for a few years, doing the best they knew how. But God's discipline is always good for us, so that we might share in his holiness.
11 No discipline is enjoyable while it is happening—it's painful! But afterward there will be a peaceful harvest of right living for those who are trained in this way.

Hebrews 12: 7-11

"Chew the meat and spit out the bones!" was the eating advice I received as a child when ravenously ripping apart fish. "Chewing the meat" and "spitting out the bones" allowed me to place an entire piece of food in my mouth, keep the meat I wanted to eat and then spit out the bones I didn't want. Chew the enjoyable; spit out the difficult. It seems that we've taken that concept from the kitchen to Christ. We lick our lips at God's blessings and then suck our teeth at God's requirements. It now seems that we chew the blessings and spit out the expectations. Family, God loves you as you are but will not accept you where you're at. His expectation is that we mature from heathenism to holiness. The highway from sinner to saint is paved through the rough road of sanctification. Might I take you on a tour inside "God's Correctional Facility?"

The author of the Book of Hebrews is often debated, but the purpose is not: *faith is our foundation.* The author performs a 13-chapter x-ray on faith, to ensure believers that believing God is more important than seeing God. In fact, we are reared by records of believers who died for God without having seen God. Faith was Moses' GPS. Faith was Noah's blue print. Faith was Sarah's in-vitro fertilization. Through the book of Hebrews, God

"It takes faith to do what God requires even when you can't see why He requires it."

wanted us to know that faith is the stairway up which heaven in climbed. The book's anthem might very well be found in Hebrews 11:1, *"Faith is the substance of things hoped for, and the evidence of things not seen."* It takes faith to do *what* God requires even when you can't see *why* He requires it.

So Lawrence, why then this passage on enduring correction? Why not tell us about the "big things" people used their faith to accomplish?

Why not tell us about Cain and Abel? Or Moses and the Promised Land? Or Noah and the Ark? They all used their faith to achieve greatness for God. Why this passage on enduring correction? I'm glad you asked! Family, you can't achieve like these people achieved until you believe like these people believed, and what they all have in common is that they allowed themselves to be corrected by God. *Got endurance?*

The Bible is a 66-track love song between a holy God and a heathen people. God desires our salvation but requires our purification. We cannot be made perfect through our own might, but through our submission to God's will and God's way. Simply said, that is going to require us to clean up our acts! The text not only tells us of the necessity of God's correction, but it also tells us of its nature:

➢ *Correction is an act of love: "As you endure this divine discipline, remember that God is treating you as his own children. Who ever heard of a child who is never disciplined by its father?"* The conflagration of fatherless households has made correction and discipline foreign concepts, but trust that correction comes from care not contempt. One of the most enduring symbols of Jesus is Him as a shepherd holding a staff. Ever notice the hook at the head of the staff? Whenever sheep drifted from the pasture, the shepherd slipped the loop over the sheep's neck and returned them back to the path. Though it felt like a chokehold, it was really a loving gesture. Get it?

➤ *Correction is an act of inclusion:* *"If God doesn't discipline you as he does all of his children, it means that you are illegitimate and are not really his children at all."* If you do not allow God to correct you like a child, how do you expect to call Him your father? The text uses the term "illegitimate child" in the New Living Translation but in the King James Version the text refers to them as "bastards." No matter how you translate it, the meaning is the same – the black sheep stands out because they won't fit in. I don't know about you, but before I die and go to hell, I'd color myself correct!

➤ *Correction is painful but purposeful:* *"No discipline is enjoyable while it is happening—it's painful! But afterward there will be a peaceful harvest of right living for those who are trained in this way."* Joy can exist in the absence of enjoyment. Holiness is the product but correction is the process. As children of God, we must endure the cross of correction in order to accept the crown of Christ. It's like the old saying suggests, "No pain, no gain!" The Good News with God is that the gain far outweighs the pain. Go through what you're going through so you can get where you're going to! God uses pain to polish us in preparation for His promises.

As we mature, we become sober in recognizing that living for God is not easy. It is not like hitting the lottery, punching in the right combination of praises and paying my tithes straight in box. It is not like Poker, where I can bluff my way into God's Full House. Living for God is unlike anything we've ever done before. God is the only person who knows us for who we TRULY are: every sin, cataloged by time and date. It's because God knows our true nature that His correction is so hard to take. We can't fool Him. He wants the habit your partner doesn't know about, the sins your parents can't stand to hear, and the past you can't stand to relive. God wants it all. It's going to be painful, but please trust that God doesn't remove without replacing. He'll trade you with you – your habits for His holiness, your past for His future, your anger for His protection, and your tears for His joy! On Calvary He traded His Son for our sins. Praise be to God!

> **Challenge Questions**
>
> *1. Which hurts more: God's private correction of my sins or God's public exposure of them?*
>
> ---
>
> *2. What areas of my life are most difficult to allow God to correct me in?*
>
> ---
>
> *3. Which do I desire more: the life I live today or the life I live tomorrow?*

Family, don't hop off the treadmill of God's correction just yet. Shed the pounds of a painful past and a sinful start. God is making you into who He needs you to be by ridding you of who you used to be. Don't spit out the bones; they belong to the new body God is building for you!

 MODERN DAY PROVERBS

Memory Verse: *For whom the LORD loveth he correcteth; even as a father the son in whom he delighteth. – Proverbs 3:12*

MODERN DAY
PROVERBS

18

Hair Today, Gone Tomorrow

The moth's problem isn't the fire;
it's his attraction to it.

Hair Today, Gone Tomorrow

4 Some time later Samson fell in love with a woman named Delilah, who lived in the valley of Sorek.

5 The rulers of the Philistines went to her and said, "Entice Samson to tell you what makes him so strong and how he can be overpowered and tied up securely. Then each of us will give you 1,100 pieces of silver."

6 So Delilah said to Samson, "Please tell me what makes you so strong and what it would take to tie you up securely."

17 Finally, Samson shared his secret with her. "My hair has never been cut," he confessed, "for I was dedicated to God as a Nazirite from birth. If my head were shaved, my strength would leave me, and I would become as weak as anyone else."

19 Delilah lulled Samson to sleep with his head in her lap, and then she called in a man to shave off the seven locks of his hair. In this way she began to bring him down, and his strength left him.

20 Then she cried out, "Samson! The Philistines have come to capture you!" When he woke up, he thought, "I will do as before and shake myself free." But he didn't realize the Lord had left him.

Judges 16: 4-6, 17, 19-20

In this passage, we encounter several excerpts from one of the Bible's most exceptional love stories. To the casual reader it would appear that the amorous assembly would consist of Samson and Delilah. In other words, you would read this passage and pardonably presume that the lovers in this story are Samson and Delilah; not so. The two main actors in this passage proceed from the same person; the true love affair here is between Samson and his own strength. Born a Nazirite, with God-given strength in his hair, Samson lost it all due to a weakness in his head. Can I pull over for a minute and sing you Samson's sad song, "Hair Today, Gone Tomorrow?"

Familiarly unfamiliar to many is the story of Samson and Delilah. Many of us loosely learned that Samson's strength was derived from his hair and that somehow his relationship with Delilah led to his strength being sapped. Well family, if the truth be told – Samson was the sap! The reason that Samson lost his God-given ability, the reason that we lose ours, is because Samson tried to pimp his abilities and got tricked!

> "The reason that Samson lost his God-given ability, the reason we lose ours, is because Samson tried to pimp his abilities and got tricked!"

Samson was a judge and notoriously noted for his great physical strength. Samson was known for once tearing apart a lion with his bare hands. There was even a time where he slayed 1,000 Philistines with the jawbone of a donkey. From Samson's very birth, an angel of the Lord appeared to his mother and foretold her of God's promise to bestow this great gift upon Samson. There was no question that Samson was endowed with God-given ability; the question becomes why did he give the world a gift that God gave him?

Samson, though physically strong, was spiritually weak. With Samson's great strength came a great responsibility *("To whom much is given, much is required")*. The messenger of the Lord stipulated that Samson's hair was never to be cut; this was the secret of his strength. If his hair was cut, he would be no more than a mortal man. Samson had God's gift, but he had to maintain God's grace; don't tell anyone where your strength comes from! Well, like many of us, Samson unwrapped his gift and left the instructions flapping in the wind. Been there? Instead of praising God with his gifts, he promoted himself. Instead of glorifying the God of Israel, Samson glorified the god of egotism. Sound like anyone you know?

Samson's strong suit was fighting but his soft spot was females. In Judges 16, we find Samson not only sleeping with the enemy, but permitting his power to be the subject of pillow talk. Delilah inquires, *"Please tell me what makes you so strong and what it would take to tie you up securely".* Samson! Were you listening? She asked what it would take to make you weak so she could tie you up! No, Samson! Noooo!!!!! Family, I don't care how fine a woman(or a man) is – *no piece is worth your power!* But here goes Samson, already lying in bed with the enemy; he then desires to play games with God's gift. Three times, Samson tricks Delilah by giving her the runaround about the true source of his strength. After much pleading though on her part, she finally convinces Samson to concede – he tells her the source of his strength. No sooner than he does, she shaves his head and he loses his strength. Samson tried to pimp God's power and ended up tricked!

Challenge Questions

1. Do I place more value in the gift than I do the Giver?

---

2. Do my talents glorify God's name or my own?

---

3. How long do I expect to prosper by prostituting God's gift for my glory?

Family, contrary to our salacious social consciousness, it is "trickin'" if you got it", because everything you got, God gave you! Have you ever been like Samson, flaunting your God-given ability before men, preferring fans to followers? Have you ever used your talent to attract attention to your strength instead of to your Source? Has it been you that has pimped God's gift by prostituting yourself? Ask me how I know? I spent the first 25 years of my life on the ho-stroll.

Samson's strength was unparalleled, but his faith was paralytic. Because Samson had high talent but low judgment, his strength was "Hair Today and Gone Tomorrow." Samson was powerful one day then puny the next. Prima Donna one day then Persona Non-Grata the next.

You should know that Samson's hair did eventually grow back

and he regained his strength, but by that time, he was a slave to the Philistines and relegated to grinding grain. In his final feat of strength he tears down the pillars of the palace and dies with his enemies. Samson died in his mess; I pray that you do not.

Family, if you're ready to get off the corner and into Christ, why not make today the day?

Memory Verse: *You must worship no other gods, for the Lord, whose very name is Jealous, is a God who is jealous about his relationship with you. – Exodus 10:14*

MODERN DAY

PROVERBS

19

Upon Further Review

Knowing where you're going to can help you with what you're going through.

Upon Further Review

19 So the two of them continued on their journey. When they came to Bethlehem, the entire town was excited by their arrival. "Is it really Naomi?" the women asked.
20 "Don't call me Naomi," she responded. "Instead, call me Mara, for the Almighty has made life very bitter for me.
21 I went away full, but the Lord has brought me home empty. Why call me Naomi when the Lord has caused me to suffer and the Almighty has sent such tragedy upon me?"
22 So Naomi returned from Moab, accompanied by her daughter-in-law Ruth, the young Moabite woman. They arrived in Bethlehem in late spring, at the beginning of the barley harvest.

Ruth 1:19-22

       Instant replay – since 1986 it has been the NFL's answer to human error and missed calls made by game officials. Due to the fast-paced nature of the game of football, several referees were making errant calls, not intentionally but because the human eye doesn't see everything. Often times, what they thought they saw wasn't always what actually occurred. As a way to correct this concern, in the case of "questionable calls," the NFL allowed officials to call "timeouts" and go to a booth to review the play on the field. "Upon Further Review" they were able to see the play on the field once more, from another perspective, and then make a new determination based on this second examination. Given a second chance to review the play, referees were granted the opportunity to judge the play accurately, seeing in some cases, what they were unable to see the first time. Family, I'd like to call a "timeout" in your life, and ask you to join me in the booth – "Upon Further Review" your situation may not be so bad.

> "... in the Jewish culture it is a point of shame for a woman to be a widow and/or lose her sons..."

The book of Ruth, aptly named after its heroine, starts principally portraying her mother-in-law Naomi's tragic story of loss. Naomi left her home in Bethlehem with her husband to move to the foreign country of Moab to start her new life and new family. For a time, life was joyous and full. That would soon change, however. In just 10 short years, Naomi would suffer not only the loss of her husband, but also both her sons; talk about an extreme home makeover. In just 10 short years, Naomi literally went from rags to riches. It's important to note the familial and sociological loss for Naomi: in the Jewish culture it is a point of shame for a woman to be a widow and/or lose her sons(her ability to birth another generation; here, Naomi lost BOTH.

Dissonant, despondent, and disappointed, Naomi dismisses her two daughters-in-law, Ruth and Orpah and effectually tells them to cut their losses and move on with their lives. While Orpah takes the severance package, Ruth begs Naomi to return home to Bethlehem with her and Naomi reluctantly agrees. Naomi, now accompanied by Ruth, reaches the outskirts of her hometown when she is identified by a townswoman who shouts, *"Isn't that Naomi?"* Dejected and depressed, Naomi makes a determination about her situation and responds, *"Don't call me Naomi, call me Mara (the Jewish word meaning "bitter") because the Lord has dealt with me bitterly. I left home full, but the Lord has sent me home empty."* Based on her sociological assessment, through the cataract of her confusion, Naomi made a call on the field of her future – "Don't call me Naomi, call me Mara (bitter)."

Ever been there? Has the pain and pressure of a poor situation caused you to feel poorly about yourself? Have you stood in Naomi's shoes, so secluded in your sadness that you feel like even God has left you? I've been there too, but let's call a timeout and review this play from God's perspective.

In the person of Ruth, God would give Naomi a second chance at life. As the story goes, Ruth would sit under Naomi's learning tree and eventually wed a man, Boaz, a kinsman of Naomi, that would redeem and restore righteousness back to Naomi's lineage. The child's name would be called Obed, Obed would give birth to Jesse and Jesse would give birth to a cat I think you may know: His name was David! You see, at the very time that Naomi called her situation *"bitter,"* God was working out a "sweet" outcome: Ruth was standing right next to her! "Upon Further Review" God hadn't fumbled Naomi's fortune; Naomi had simply lost sight. Naomi made a sociological assessment of her situation but failed to take spiritual inventory. Her men had died, but her God still lived! Her resources were depleted but her Redeemer still lived! "Upon Further Review," Naomi was able to see that the ruling on the field still stands – *God is good!*

Family, I dare you to review your current condition. It may seem as if the world around you is falling apart, but if you've got faith in God, you can look at life from a different angle and perhaps see what you didn't see before. Remember – the Christian doesn't suffer any less than the rest of the world; we just see suffering differently. The world can only see what they're going through; the Believer sees where they're going to! I beg you, call a timeout in your life. Allow God to rewind the play on the field and show you what you didn't see before - He's been with you ALL ALONG.

Challenge Questions

1. How can a different perspective produce a different attitude in my life?

---

2. Will I let difficult times determine my disposition?

---

3. What are some situations in my life I can see differently, "Upon Further Review"?

~140~

 Upon Further Review

"Upon Further Review" you will find that the ruling in the world STILL STANDS – Jesus is Lord!

Memory Verse: *I have been young, and now am old; yet have I not seen the righteous forsaken, nor his seed begging bread. – Psalm 37:25*

MODERN DAY

PROVERBS

20

Faith: God's Corrective Lenses

I n life, there are some things you have to close
your eyes to see.

Faith: God's Corrective Lenses

22 When they arrived at Bethsaida, some people brought a blind man to Jesus, and they begged him to touch the man and heal him.
23 Jesus took the blind man by the hand and led him out of the village. Then, spitting on the man's eyes, he laid his hands on him and asked, "Can you see anything now?"
24 The man looked around. "Yes," he said, "I see people, but I can't see them very clearly. They look like trees walking around."
25 Then Jesus placed his hands on the man's eyes again, and his eyes were opened. His sight was completely restored, and he could see everything clearly.

Mark 8: 22-25

Vision: 1. a manifestation to the senses of something immaterial 2. the act or power of seeing : SIGHT

Ever take an eye exam? Is there a fate in all the world any worse? Does this sound familiar?

The Optometrist: "Read the first line."
You (with confidence):   "E!"

The Optometrist: "Now the next line"

You (louder than the first time, insulted at the line of questioning):
"F-P!!"

You're solid, certain, and cocky for the first couple of lines but then come the bottom rows:

The Optometrist: "Now THIS line"

You (nervous and now squinting): "Uh…E….O…Uh…T…3…Uh, can I buy a vowel?!"

The Optometrist: "Well, it looks like you're gonna need glasses!"

The doctor then leaves to fit you with corrective lenses that will improve your ability to see things more clearly. Well family, with Jesus it's the same way. Let me tell you about "Faith: God's Corrective Lenses."

Here in Mark 8, we find Jesus, the Ontological Optometrist, hard at work. Jesus is conducting a spiritual eye exam with a blind man from Bethsaida. The blind man's friends brought him to Jesus in hopes that Jesus would restore his sight. His friends had faith, but Jesus wasn't satisfied with the faith around him; He wanted to examine the faith within him. *I could preach right there.* Family, God is not interested in your prayin' husband/wife/pastor/friend/co-worker/tv preacher/tarot card reader – they might carry you to the altar but you've got to stand on your own! Jesus examined this man's spiritual eyesight before He addressed his physical eyesight.

Notice Jesus' approach. Different than other healings, He only healed the man partially. Jesus paused in the middle of the exam and asked Him to 'read the next line,' to which he answered, "Yes." He said, "I see people, but I can't see them very clearly. They look like trees walking around." Clearly this blind brother was bugging: people, who look like trees?! His vision was still blurry. Jesus had not yet given Him full sight. Wait: was Jesus unable to perform a complete miracle? Was Jesus out of healing ability? The intelligent question is, Jesus, why did you only give him partial sight? Well, I'm glad you asked! The answer and our lesson lie here.

"...Jesus, WHY did you only give [the blind man] partial sight?"

Faith and vision go hand in hand. God calls us to believe first, then see. If you can't believe, you can't see. The reason most of us have "blurry vision" is because we have "blurry faith." The blind man became the blurry man not because Jesus had limited power, but because he had limited faith. My brothers and sisters, you can't achieve greatly unless you believe greatly.

The Holy Book is littered with passages on faith, sight, and God's pleasure:

> **Challenge Questions**
>
> *1. What areas of my life am I unable to see clearly?*
>
> ---
>
> *2. Might the "fog" have something to do with my faith?*
>
> ---
>
> *3. How can I recover my spiritual sight?*

Hebrews 11:1 – Now faith is the substance of things hoped for, the evidence of things not seen.

Hebrews 11:6 - But without faith it is impossible to please him: for he that cometh to God must believe that he is, and that he is a rewarder of them that diligently seek him.

Mark 9:23 - Jesus said unto him, If thou canst believe, all things are possible to him that believeth.

The blind man recovered his sight AFTER he recovered his faith. Jesus didn't ask him "what" he could see; He asked him "if" he could see. The man confessed and professed at the same time, "Yes, I see people." The blind man started to believe that Jesus was starting to do something great in his life. At that confession, Jesus filled his prescription. Jesus granted him full sight AFTER he exhibited full faith. Plain language y'all –

if you want to be more, believe more. Faith is God's Corrective Lens; the more God you're able to believe, the more God you'll be able to see.

Should you need a prescription, I know a Physician.

Memory Verse: *Now faith is the substance of things hoped for, the evidence of things not seen. – Hebrews 11:1*

MODERN DAY

PROVERBS

21

Clean Water and Dirty Filters

It's pretty hard to serve a clean God on a dirty plate.

Clean Water and Dirty Filters

7 People can tame all kinds of animals, birds, reptiles, and fish, but no one can tame the tongue. It is restless and evil, full of deadly poison.
8 Sometimes it praises our Lord and Father, and sometimes it curses those who have been made in the image of God. And so blessing and cursing come pouring out of the same mouth.
9 Surely, my brothers and sisters, this is not right!
10 Does a spring of water bubble out with <u>both fresh water and bitter water</u>?
11 Does a fig tree produce olives, or a grapevine produce figs?
12 No, and you can't draw fresh water from a salty spring.

James 3:7-12

A household chore taught me a profound spiritual lesson. I have a pet turtle named Hannah*(my daughter named her, not me)*, and I was changing the water in her tank. For those of you who may not know, turtles are the filthiest of all semi-aquatic animals and the most difficult to keep clean. Their very physiology sets the stage for their filth; they have the innate ability to eat and defecate at the same time. No sooner does food go in then *"poop"* comes out. Their water gets dirty so quickly that turtle tanks require a filter to keep the water clean, preventing toxins in the water from killing the turtles. In essence, the filter keeps them from dying in their own *"mess."*

I removed my turtle from her tank, cleaned the tank and replenished it with new water but noticed that the water got dirty again almost instantly. What went wrong? The water was clean and the turtle was out? Why was my water dirty again? God spoke to me as clear as day: "Your filter is dirty, and you can't produce clean water with a dirty filter."

> *"Much like the turtle is the filthiest member of semi-aquatic animals, the human tongue is the filthiest member of the human body."*

My household chore became a modern day proverb. Let me talk to you from the subject, "Clean Water & Dirty Filters."

Much like the turtle is the filthiest member of semi-aquatic animals, the human tongue is the filthiest member of the human body. James describes the tongue in verse 7 as, "restless and evil, full of deadly poison." This may seem harsh when read between the holy pages of scripture but it's a reality when you live at the hellish intersection of "Keepin' It" St. & "Real" Blvd. Face it, our mouths are nasty. We talk dirty talk and eat dirty things. We eat everything and talk about anything. We'll put anything in our mouths – new nonsense, old gossip, corroded conversation, new lies, used partners – we'll put *EVERYTHING and ANYTHING* in our mouths. The consequence of original sin has predisposed our flesh to such corruption, which is why

the Bible says that we are "born in sin and shaped in iniquity." We must become conscious and honest enough to recognize that we were made from dirt and sometimes act dirty.

James proposes the problem with our vulgar vice in verses 9 and 10 when he says,

> *"Sometimes it praises our Lord and Father, and sometimes it curses those who have been made in the image of God. And so blessing and cursing come pouring out of the same mouth. Surely, my brothers and sisters, this is not right!"*

God our Father cannot accept our "dirty" water. When we give in to cursing and vulgarity, we contaminate God's most prized tool, our mouths. Consider David when he says, "I will bless the Lord at all times and His praise shall continually be in my mouth." How can the waters of God's blessing and the sludge of our cursing exist in the same well? James waxes poetically about this issue in verse 11 when he asks, "Does a spring of water bubble out with both fresh water and bitter water?" Family, we can't have it both ways; it's got to be praise or profanity, but not both. Would we dare ask God to drink His pristine praises from the inside of our feces-filled cups?

Here's the practical point – our mouth is God's vessel and our mind is the filter. The cleanliness of the "water" that flows out from our mouths is dependant upon the cleanliness of the "filter." Dirty mind, dirty mouth. Clean mind; clean mouth. Cloudy mind, cloudy mouth. Whatever you conceive on the inside WILL be born on the outside. This is why Jesus says in Matthew 12:34, "for out of the abundance of the heart the mouth speaketh." If you want to clean the "water" your mouth produces, you've got to clean the filter. Much like a criminal on the lamb, we must apprehend and arrest every thought leads to unrighteousness.

The challenge for many of us is that we're trying to be clean in a dirty place. We're trying to be clean with dirty friends, married with dirty partners, or employed with dirty co-workers. Like a dirty filter placed in a tank of clean water, it will only be a matter of time before the water is dirty again.

> **Challenge Questions**
>
> 1. Would you eat off the floor?
>
> ---
>
> 2. Would you kiss someone who ate off the floor?
>
> ---
>
> 3. Would God accept praise that's been on the floor?

The Bible gives us several Scriptures to help us "clean our filters."

➤ *Renew Your Mind* - "And be not conformed to this world: but be ye transformed by the renewing of your mind, that ye may prove what is that good, and acceptable, and perfect, will of God." – Romans 12:2

➤ *Tame Your Tempter* - "Be ye angry, and sin not: let not the sun go

down upon your wrath." – Ephesians 4:26

➢ *Mind Your Company* - "Blessed is the man that walketh not in the counsel of the ungodly, nor standeth in the way of sinners, nor sitteth in the seat of the scornful." – Psalm 1:1

Please let me testify when I confess that this is my greatest area of challenge. I am often tempted to curse folks out. I grew up listening to more Eddie Murphy than I did T.D. Jakes, so I'm more inclined to quote lines from "Raw" than from the Bible. I'm working at it and I know you are, too.

As a child of God, my goal is not to be "holier than thou", just better than I used to be. Remember today that we are God's ambassadors; the Jesus they see in us will be the Jesus they see in themselves.

It's pretty tough to serve a clean God on a dirty plate.

Memory Verse: *So set yourselves apart to be holy, for I am the Lord your God. - Leviticus 20:7*

Humility is an effective hearing aid. People tend to listen more when you talk less.

God's Wrapping Paper

God's Wrapping Paper

24 Then they began to argue among themselves about who would be the greatest among them.
25 Jesus told them, "In this world the kings and great men lord it over their people, yet they are called 'friends of the people.' 26 But among you it will be different. Those who are the greatest among you should take the lowest rank, and the leader should be like a servant. 27 Who is more important, the one who sits at the table or the one who serves? The one who sits at the table, of course. But not here! For I am among you as one who serves.

Luke 22:24-27

What do the Spanish Inquisition, the Oprah Winfrey Show, and your family's holiday dinner table all have in common? They are all places where you can expect to be interrogated, interviewed, and evaluated! What kind of work do you do now? So, who are you dating now? So, how's the marriage? Ahh!!!!! The family dining room has become a talk show that most of us don't want to be guests on. So bent on serving the god called approval, we often lead with our best foot, lie with the best intention, and flaunt our gifts for our families. The holidays at home look more like fashion shows, career fairs, and debate forums. God didn't intend for us to flaunt our gifts for gain-sake and parade our purpose for prestige. Can I talk to you for a moment about "God's Wrapping Paper?"

Our text finds Jesus and His disciples at the table of the Last Supper. Jesus prepared a meal to prepare His followers for the time that was to come. Jesus, who was their Teacher, their Leader, and their Lord, took this opportunity to teach them a great lesson in humility. In verse 24, an argument breaks out amongst the disciples as to who the "greatest" of them would be. Here they were, at the table of the Lord's Supper, sitting together with Jesus for the final time, and here they were bickering. *Sound familiar?* They had gotten so wrapped up in themselves that they lost sight of the fact that Jesus was not only in their midst, but had prepared a meal just for them. Family, this is the problem with infighting: we get so wrapped up in ourselves that we lose sight of Jesus. Our fellowship turns to fighting, our bonds to bickering, and our power into pettiness. This would be the last time that all 12 disciples ate together, and here they were, fighting big over little stuff!

> *"... this is the problem with infighting: we get so wrapped up in ourselves that we lose sight of Jesus."*

Jesus interrogatively intervenes and poses the question: "Who is more important, the one who sits at the table or the one who serves?" Jesus was asking them whether it was more powerful to be the "servant" or the "served." the prince or the pauper, the garbage collector or the CEO? Their response, and all too often ours, would esteem the person of power. Jesus sharply disagreed for He says, "not here!" Jesus wanted them to understand that not only at His table, but also in His Father's kingdom that no glory would be assigned to the "high and mighty." Jesus wanted it to be painfully clear that "the first shall be last, and the last shall be first." Jesus used His service as His sermon and said to them, "For I am among you as the one who serves."

In these, the final days of Jesus' journey, He demonstrated unparalleled humility and service to His friends. Jesus washed their feet, served them dinner, and ultimately laid down His life for them. Jesus, the Son of God, from birth until death wrapped His gifts in humility.

> ### Challenge Questions
>
> *1. What drives your climb up the success ladder: personal satisfaction or public approval?*
>
> ---
>
> *2. How much more effective could my service be if I wrapped my gifts in humility?*
>
> ---
>
> *3. Who do I alienate when I boast? Have I lowered someone else privately by elevating myself publicly?*

Jesus' entire life was about humility. He was born in a manger, wrapped in funeral rags. He dwelled among the lowly. He charged many that He healed to tell no one. He forgave sins. He restored the ear of His arresting officer, and ultimately He died alone. The Son of God, the Savior of the world embodied power yet served with humility. As Jesus bled and died on the cross, His first words were still altruistic, "Father forgive them, for they know not what they do." From His first second, right until His final hour, Jesus our King crowned Himself in humility. I am fully persuaded that this is the wrapping paper in which God wants us to display our gifts. Please be proud of your accomplishments but don't rob God of the glory and your family of the fellowship in the meantime.

The dinner table will be full enough this Christmas; why not leave your ego at home? Your salary can't save you, your degree doesn't define you, and your occupation shouldn't preoccupy you. Jesus didn't bring His resumé to the Last Supper; don't bring yours to the dinner table.

Memory Verse: *Those who are the greatest among you should take the lowest rank, and the leader should be like a servant. – Luke 22:26*

MODERN DAY

PROVERBS

23

Your Past: A Present to Your Future

God can use the pain of your past to propel you into your future. Low places today; launching pads tomorrow!

Your Past: A Present to Your Future

28 And we know that God causes everything to work together for the good of those who love God and are called according to his purpose for them.

Romans: 8:28

"God, Why Me?" is the sullen song sung by those who have been used, abused, and refused by the Rhythm & Blues album we call Life. Fairly or unfairly, life has caused us to experience pain, frustration, and straight up disappointment that we are certain God didn't intend. *"God, Why Me? Why me with the past and the problems? Why me with the pain and the parents? Why me with the perversion and the promiscuity? God, Why Me?!"* Not only "Why" the problems God, but "What" God is the purpose behind my problems and my past? I'm so glad you asked; let me assure you that "Your past is a present to your future!"

Paul directs this text message to an audience in Rome who were deeply concerned that their past was going to catch up with them. For some it was the active sins they committed, for others it was the passive sins they allowed, yet for some still it wasn't what they did, but what was done to them. Sinners desired salvation, believers desired confirmation,

and Paul provided them both with emancipation by declaring that, *"God causes everything to work together for the good."* Now that's Good News! Every scar you've suffered, every bump that's bruised you, every mistake you've made – God is able to cause EVERYTHING to work for your good!

Many of us have trouble believing that because we don't see how God could make a miracle out of a mess. Well, shall we do a roll call of the Bible: Moses was a stutterer, Noah was a senior citizen, Jonah was a racist, David was a murderer and an adulterer, Ezekiel was a Looney Tune (he once talked to dead bones), Jeremiah was a cry baby, Peter was a punk, and Paul was a stuffed-shirt. God majors in using minor people! There was nothing special about Mary; she wasn't the only virgin in town. There was nothing special about Elizabeth(John the Baptist's mom), she wasn't the only old barren woman in town. Rather, God uses whomever and whatever however He pleases to accomplish His will. Don't worry God about what you've been through; focus on where God is taking you to!

> "God uses whomever and whatever, however He pleases to accomplish His will.

God would become Moses' Speech Pathologist, Noah's Red Bull, Jonah's Interventionist, David's Confession Booth, Ezekiel's Prozac, Jeremiah's Kleenex, Peter's Courage, Paul's New Testament, Mary's Baby Daddy, and Elizabeth's In-Vitro Fertilization! God causes EVERYTHING to work together for our good!

Paul assures us today that *"God causes EVERYTHING to work together for the good."* Paul would know that fact personally. Paul, (formerly Saul) was a law-keeping, self-righteous, murderous man. Yet, in spite of his past, God used him to lead legions to Christ, using the knowledge he had acquired from his past. Paul would use his previously acquired knowledge of the Jewish laws to lead many Jews and Gentiles to Christ.

Family, hear God's voice today – EVERYTHING will work together for your good! Your past – it will work! Your pain – it will work! Your problem – it will work! Everything will work for your good; not because life intended it, but because God wills it so!

In reflecting on this passage, I often look back at my own life and see this text profoundly evident and prophetically relevant. The most painful parts of my past are now the source of my power. The very life experiences that God has brought me through, He is now using me to bring others through. The very jobs I hated working, He now uses the skills I acquired then to bless me now.

> ### Challenge Questions
>
> *1. Will I allow the pain that robbed me of my past to rob me of my future?*
>
> ---
>
> *2. What can I tell God about me that He doesn't already know?*
>
> ---
>
> *3. What kinds of opportunities is my past preventing me from?*

The very people I couldn't stand being around then, are the very people who hail me now. I'm living proof – God causes EVERYTHING to work for the good!

If you want to understand the purpose behind the pain, might I refer you to the God with the plan? God is the only one who can show you how "Your Past is a Present to your Future!"

Memory Verse: *No, dear brothers and sisters, I have not achieved it, but I focus on this one thing: Forgetting the past and looking forward to what lies ahead. – Philippians 3:13*

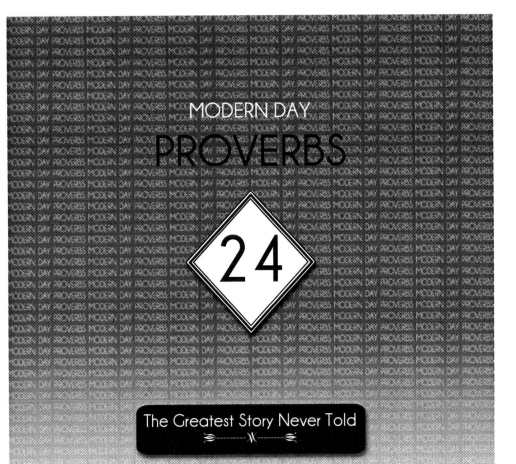

Success isn't promised: opportunity is.

The Greatest Story Never Told

¹⁴*For the kingdom of heaven is as a man traveling into a far country, who called his own servants, and delivered unto them his goods.*
¹⁵*And unto one he gave five talents, to another two, and to another one; to every man according to his several ability; and straightway took his journey.*
¹⁶*Then he that had received the five talents went and traded with the same, and made them other five talents.*
¹⁷*And likewise he that had received two, he also gained other two.*
¹⁸*But he that had received one went and digged in the earth, and hid his lord's money.*

Matthew 25: 14-18

Ever wonder what separates winners from losers, succeeding from failing? I guarantee you that it has nothing to do with what God's giving you, but has everything to with what you're giving God. Success isn't promised; opportunity is.

In this parable from Matthew, Jesus is again describing the kingdom of heaven to His disciples. He describes heaven as a "man traveling into a far country"(ever wonder how far heaven was from your house?!), who distributed his possessions to his servants(namely, us). To one he gave five talents, to another he gave two talents, and yet another he gave one talent. And as the story goes, the servant with five multiplied his five, the servant with two multiplied his two – but this last servant, the one who only received one talent(poor baby) threw a tantrum and hid his talent in the dirt! Sadly, the story of this servant's accomplishment and talent was never told. Sound familiar? Too many of us roam the earth bitter and beleaguered, while our talent decays – buried in the dirt.

> "If you only knew what God went through to give you what you have, you'd do more with what you've got!"

Though these servants all received a different amount of talent, what they have in common is that they ALL got something! Not only that, they received something they did not deserve from a "man" that traveled so very far to bring it to them! If you only knew what God went through to give you what you have, you'd do more with what you've got! We know the story of the man with five talents, and the story of the man with two talents, but sadly the story of the man with one talent is – "The Greatest Story NEVER Told!"

Too many of us sit at the distribution center of God's blessings, and instead of appreciating and utilizing the talents that God gave us, we whine and compare our talent to those that God gave someone else. Shameful, but so common. Beloved, you should know that the fastest way to lose what God gave you is to worry about what God gave someone else!

Before we get too far gone, let's remember a couple of things about this parable:

> No matter how many talents you have, the same God gives them all.

> You didn't have any talent before God gave them to you; anything is an improvement.

> You're in possession of talent, but you don't own it. Failing to use it is actually stealing from God.

Challenge Questions

1. Am I truly appreciative of the gifts God gave me or am I comparing them to someone else's? Remember, you can't weigh your worth on someone else's scale.

---

2. What do I have in common with successful, wise, and wealthy people? The SAME God makes you all.

---

3. Will I have an acceptable return on God's investment before the "market" closes? You'd better; because where God can't get multiplication, there will be division!

Sadly, some of the world's greatest stories have never been told. Maybe it's the inner city kid who feels like they never got the opportunities other kid's got; depressed, they forfeit any and all opportunities God sends his or her way. Maybe it's the youngest sibling who's in college with the undecided major, freezing in the shadows of his or her older siblings' success. Perhaps it's the young minister who's jealous of the anointing God gave his or her peers, blindly aborting their own. Fill in your own situation here, but the question is the same – what's keeping your story out of the history books? Certainly it's not God's fault. Go grab a shovel, find that place in the dirt, and recover your talent!

"Opportunity is a pen, talent the ink, and life your book – God will publish if you'll write!" – L. Alexander

My brother, my sister, I challenge you to search yourself and inquire – what am I doing with the talent God gave me? It may not be as much as God gave someone else, but it's more than enough for me, and if God gave it to me, then who am I to block His blessing? Some of the world's greatest stories may NEVER be told – don't add your manuscript to the scrap heap. Talent is God's gift to us; what we do with our talent is our gift to God. What are you giving God?

Memory Verse: *When someone has been given much, much will be required in return; and when someone has been entrusted with much, even more will be required. – Luke 12:48b*

MODERN DAY

PROVERBS

25

Why Jesus Needed Judas

D on't sacrifice 11 disciples on account of 1 Judas.

Why Jesus Needed Judas

1 -4 The prayer was no sooner prayed than it was answered. Jesus called twelve of his followers and sent them into the ripe fields. He gave them power to kick out the evil spirits and to tenderly care for the bruised and hurt lives. This is the list of the twelve he sent:

Simon (they called him Peter, or "Rock"),
Andrew, his brother,
James, Zebedee's son,
John, his brother,
Philip,
Bartholomew,
Thomas,
Matthew, the tax man,
James, son of Alphaeus,
Thaddaeus,
Simon, the Canaanite,
Judas Iscariot (who later turned on him).

Matthew 10:1-4 (The Message Translation)

Consider the Twelve Disciples, the starting lineup for Jesus' public ministry. He prayed to His Father for 12 hands to help Him with the "harvest" of souls that would soon be won. This carefully casted crew consisted of "The Rock" Simon Peter, the "Sons of Thunder" James and John, "Mr. IRS" Matthew, and several others that rounded out this almighty all-star team. The question many of us have is – Lord, why Judas? This is the traitor who sold you out for thirty silver pieces. Not only that, he would kiss you before he dissed you. Jesus – why Judas? Well, pull up a chair family and let me tell you "Why Jesus Needed Judas."

"...don't be so quick to throw out the "Judas" in your camp..."

Let's just be practical and give Judas his due:

➤ He was good with money – he was the accountant for the Disciples' treasury.

➤ He was the most educated of the Disciples.

➤ He was a noted negotiator(later evidenced by his betrayal of Jesus).

Family, don't be so quick to throw out the "Judas" in your camp; they

have some practical use!

Let's be scriptural and give Jesus His due:

> *Jesus was the fulfillment of Old Testament prophecy* – Jesus had to live, serve, and die according to Scripture; that required that one of His own would betray Him. More than that, Judas' betrayal of Jesus in the flesh only served to exalt Jesus' dominion in the Spirit. Jesus' resurrection would prove to the other 11 and the rest of the world that He was Lord!

> *Jesus knew Judas was a traitor from the beginning* – when you know your opposition, you can play your position. Jesus only allowed Judas to be as close to Him as He desired. He also knew Judas' tricks, so He wasn't surprised by His betrayal.

Challenge Questions

1. Do I allow the Judas in my camp to detract my attention from the rest of my team?

---

2. How can I put my Judas to work for me?

---

3. Who can Judas truly hurt but himself/herself?

> *Jesus had a larger goal to accomplish* – He still had 11 other disciples

through whom His Father's will had to be accomplished. Life lesson: don't leave your 11 on account of 1 Judas!

Here are some things you should know about the life of this Judas to help you deal with YOUR Judas:

➤ *Judas' setup led to his downfall* – the guilt Judas experienced after betraying Jesus caused him to commit suicide under a juniper tree. Don't worry about your enemies – they can't harm you; they can only harm themselves!

Many of us have a Judas in our midst: a co-worker in a cubicle, a teammate in the huddle, a family member at the dinner table, or perhaps a mate in our marriage. We all have a Judas in our midst. Maybe it's the friend who lied on you or the boss who fired you or the family member who disowned you. What they thought they were doing to curse you actually blessed you! Judas didn't sentence Jesus to death; He certified his ascension to heaven! None of us would be here today if it were not for Jesus, delivered to the cross by Judas. We actually ought to thank God for Judas, too!

Betrayal and heartache often do what pure motivation cannot. Racism was Martin's preaching power, Injustice was Ghandi's good foot, and "Can't" made Barack say "Yes We Can!"

Remember though, that much like Jesus, *Judas can't hurt you*

nearly as much as he hurts himself, so let him fulfill his purpose in your life! Kiss me, curse me, hold me, punch me, accept me, reject me – do whatever you'd like! Judas ensures that we'll see Jesus!

Judas propelled Jesus into His destiny, and counted His cash along the way. Don't let your "Judas" work you today; put your "Judas" to work for you!

Memory Verse: *When the wicked, even mine enemies and my foes, came upon me to eat up my flesh, they stumbled and fell. - Psalm 27:2*

MODERN DAY

PROVERBS

26

Jesus Solves Our "Drinking Problem"

D emanding the wrong supply and supplying the wrong demand are fatal economics.

Jesus Solves Our "Drinking" Problem

13 Jesus replied, "Anyone who drinks this water will soon become thirsty again. 14 But those who drink the water I give will never be thirsty again. It becomes a fresh, bubbling spring within them, giving them eternal life."
15 "Please, sir," the woman said, "give me this water! Then I'll never be thirsty again, and I won't have to come here to get water."

John 4:13-15

C'mon...C'mon...Don't be shy – what's your drink of choice? Is it Hennessy VSOP or is it Bacardi Dark? Neither? Ok, let me try again – is it Absolut or is it Tequila? Smirnoff Ice or Grey Goose? Corona or Bud Light? Dark liquor or light liquor? 40oz or a shot glass? In the club or in your room? Somewhere, sometime – someone has had a "drinking" problem!

Not you, huh? Well, let me try again. Have you ever gotten drunk off the malt liquor love of an abusive mate? Or taken shots of neglect so long that you could check off "married" and "single" and BOTH be true? Have you ever had to belly up to the bar of battery, balancing yourself on the legs of common sense and uncommon conditions? No matter your "drink of choice," we've all suffered from a "drinking" problem of some sort. I just wanted to warm this Gospel Happy Meal up in your microwave and tell you that "Jesus can solve your drinking problem!"

Our story in the Gospel according to John is one of the more controversial stories ever told because it finds Jesus in conversation with a prostitute. So many readers have gotten fancy and fickle and prejudged this woman's plight because she was a prostitute, but can I keep it funky like morning breath? We've all prostituted at some point, for someone or something! A prostitute exchanges their body for compensation; in other words, they give something to get something. *Prostitute, noun – it is a person, place or thing.* I don't care how long you've been saved or how long you've been sinning – ALL of us, at some point have been *with a "person", been in a "place", or have done a "thing"* that we're not quite proud of!

"We've ALL prostituted at some point, for someone or something!"

This Samaritan woman had 5 husbands plus a boo-boo that she was shackin' up with at the time. Don't judge her; at least she married the men she laid with! (yeah, I thought so). So let's give this sister and her story a chance; Jesus did.

This young sister had been in and out of relationship after relationship, in and out of love, esteemed and despised, accepted and rejected – and for every man she had, she found herself visiting this well. Jacob's Well was the town's well, and as was tradition, women went to the well to draw water for their homes as well as their men. Drawing water was by no means a pleasant experience. The well was a public well and in order to draw water, this Samaritan sister would have to endure the sinister side eyes, cuffed-mouth conversations, and all the indignation that came with being a "woman with a reputation." Had she had it her way, she'd never come to that well again, but she had no choice – she was thirsty. I find it interesting that she not only thirsted physically, but she also thirsted spiritually. This sister needed more than what that well could provide –she needed the Living Water!

Here we find our heroine, again visiting the well to drink. This was a day like any other day, or so she thought. She was prepared to deal with the drama. She was prepared to deal with the name calling. She was prepared to suffer the indignation of her situation, but she wasn't prepared for what happened next – Jesus showed up in her life!

Jesus appeared out of what seemed like nowhere to bring this sister something that was unlike anything she'd ever seen before. Jesus

> **Challenge Questions**
>
> 1. How tiring has it become to drink at someone else's well?
>
> ---
>
> 2. Is the "water" even meeting my needs anymore? Is it making me "thirstier" than before I drank it?
>
> ---
>
> 3. When will I allow Jesus to turn my parched predicament into a well spring of joy? Am I ready to get off the "bottle?"

knew what her real problem was. It wasn't that she got "thirsty"; it was that the "wells" she had been drinking from left her high and dry! The problem wasn't with her demand; it was with her supply! She had been trying to quench her thirst with the "wells of the world" – relationships, companionships, and partnerships – but all those ships sank! Jesus stepped onto the trading room floor and made her an offer she couldn't refuse – He offered her Living Water. Jesus offered her Jesus!

Jesus said to her, *"Anyone who drinks this water will soon become thirsty again. But those who drink the water I give will never be thirsty again. It becomes a fresh, bubbling spring within them, giving them eternal life."* Jesus proposed an end to her drinking problem. Jesus desired to become the man in her life – the One who could truly fill the void she'd been triaging. My brother, my sister, you should know that NO ONE will do for you what Jesus can!

Jesus' proposition was three-fold:

➤ *The "water of the world" will leave you dry* - *"Anyone who drinks this water will soon become thirsty again."* Liquor stores, drug dealers, and unhealthy partners stay in business because they can depend on our dependency. They know no matter how we complain, that – "we'll be back". If you keep "drinking" from the well you're at today, you'll be at that same well tomorrow.

> *The water Jesus' gives WILL NEVER run dry – "But those who drink the water I give will never be thirsty again."* For the Samaritan sister, that solved a couple of issues. First, she wouldn't have to endure the public shame associated with visiting the well. Secondly, she wouldn't have to subject herself to the "salty water" of sin-soaked relationships anymore.

> *She could get high on her OWN supply – "It becomes a fresh, bubbling spring within them, giving them eternal life."* This sister would no longer need that well or that man to satisfy her needs; Jesus offered her a well that would spring up within *her*. She would now be able to supply her OWN demand!

Do you want to "get off the bottle?" The bottle of bad relationships, short-lived satisfaction, and a thirsty existence – might I suggest Jesus?

Memory Verse: *Blessed are they which do hunger and thirst after righteousness: for they shall be filled. – Matthew 5:6*

MODERN DAY

PROVERBS

27

The Greatest Common Denominator

S erving God requires commitment
not consensus.

The Greatest Common Denominator

1And when the day of Pentecost was fully come, they were all with one accord in one place.

Acts 2:1

Remember Math class? It was in Ms. Puccarelli's 4th grade mathematics class that I learned a most profound numerical and now spiritual lesson. *(Coincidentally, 4th grade is the last time I got an "A" in that subject *stop laughing*).* In 4th grade, I learned about the "Greatest Common Denominator."

From what I learned of the lesson, the Greatest Common Denominator is used to reduce two or more fractions to their "lowest terms." No matter how *large the fractions were or how different the numbers appeared to be*, they all had a "common factor" that when it was applied to each of them, reduced them to their lowest existence. These numbers which were once complicated, untenable, and just plain old awkward, could actually be reduced by one "common factor" that would allow them to be used together. Once reduced, these once difficult figures were easier to use and understand. I'd just like to drop a dime into the coin slot of your spirit and tell you that *"Jesus is the Greatest Common Denominator."*

Our text in Acts 2 records the day of Pentecost. Christmas had already come, Easter passed, but now the most significant spiritual happening for the earthly continuation of Jesus' work was coming. On this day, Jesus would literally pour out His Spirit upon His disciples,

"We will NEVER access the power of the Pentecost... until we can get on ONE ACCORD."

equipping them with the tools necessary to perform His work, preach His Word, and proclaim His kingdom. While waiting on this blessed day of the Lord, the 12 disciples were found in the Upper Room, all on one accord. Twelve people, who claimed to love God, actually got together on one accord! For this disparate, diverse band of men, Jesus was the Greatest Common Denominator. These men didn't have to like each other or chill with each other - they didn't have to like each other's clothes or listen to each other's music – but they all got on one accord for the Lord's sake. They were able to receive the power of God because they were all on ONE accord.

Might I suggest that the reason many of God's people are powerless is because we've lost our Greatest Common Denominator? We will never access the power of Pentecost, and the indwelling of the Lord's Spirit, until we can get on ONE ACCORD.

Let me open a couple of windows in here:

➤ *Do you need to get along with everyone at church to serve God?* NOPE! The twelve disciples differed in nationality, personality, and occupation – yet for the sake of Jesus they got on ONE ACCORD. Church is not your massage parlor or your monster's ball – it's not there to *"make you feel good!"* The purpose of the assembly is to "serve God," not your need for a head pat.

> **Challenge Questions**
>
> *1. God isn't looking for perfect people to serve Him. Why are you?*
>
> ---
>
> *2. Which is the greater force in your life? Trust me, you can only select one:*
> *a. My need to be seen,*
> *b. My need to be heard*
> *c. My need to serve*
>
> ---
>
> *3. Why do I base my service for God on my feelings instead of my faith?*

➤ *Why can't I just "do me" and not go to church or "do me" and serve God by myself?* Remember the math lesson – you're still a fraction! Even with all of those figures added up, they still result in a fraction. The greatest sum of our collective human effort is still a fraction; the Spirit of God is what makes us whole. The best you'll ever achieve by yourself is "some."

While no monuments are created for committees, no great feats have been accomplished singularly.

➢ *Why can't God just take me like I am? He made me and He "knows my heart"!* You're right, God does know your heart, which is precisely the reason you need to get your act together! The mathematical purpose of the Greatest Common Denominator is to reduce fractions to their lowest and most comprehensible form; I suggest that the spiritual purpose is the same.

Some of us can get so high and mighty, heady and haughty, that we overcomplicate even the simplest of things, namely ourselves. Listen, it's not that deep and neither are you. Paul says in Galatians 6:3, *For if a man think himself to be something, when he is nothing, he deceiveth himself.* Stop fooling yourself – you're dust, we all are. Thank God it was dust and not dirt, because we'd be dirty instead of dusty.

My brother, my sister, take God seriously, seriously. You'll find that when you do, so much of what you thought was important truly isn't, and you'll discover that all that matters in the end is what we do for God. Stop looking for perfect people; they don't exist. You can however, serve a perfect God – He DOES exist!

If you ever truly want to experience God's power in your life, make Jesus your Greatest Common Denominator – *He may reduce you, but at least you'll be in the equation!*

MODERN DAY

PROVERBS

28

A Cold Shoulder by a Warm Fire

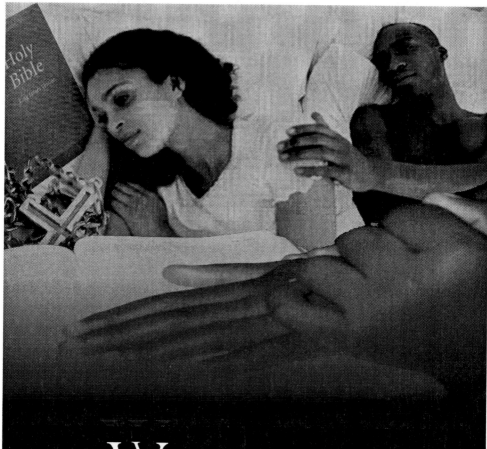

Warm hands toward the world; cold heart towards God.

A Cold Shoulder by a Warm Fire

33 Peter said, "Lord, I am ready to go to prison with you, and even to die with you."

34 But Jesus said, "Peter, let me tell you something. Before the rooster crows tomorrow morning, you will deny three times that you even know me."

55 The guards lit a fire in the middle of the courtyard and sat around it, and Peter joined them there.

56 A servant girl noticed him in the firelight and began staring at him. Finally she said, "This man was one of Jesus' followers!"

57 But Peter denied it. "Woman," he said, "I don't even know him!"

58 After a while someone else looked at him and said, "You must be one of them!" "No, man, I'm not!" Peter retorted.

59 About an hour later someone else insisted, "This must be one of them, because he is a Galilean, too."

60 But Peter said, "Man, I don't know what you are talking about." And immediately, while he was still speaking, the rooster crowed.

Luke 22: 33-34, 55-60

This must be one of the most compelling Bible stories ever told. The account of Peter's denial of Jesus reads almost bipolar and schizophrenic in nature. At one moment in time, we find Peter courageously declaring his love for Jesus by saying, "Lord, I am ready to go to prison with you, and even to die with you." Yet just one day later we find Peter cowardly denying His very affiliation with Christ, not once, but three times - "I don't even know him!" Peter possessed the power of God and love's flame when he was in Jesus' company but as soon as his company changed he exchanged loyalty for leisure. Peter gave Jesus "a cold shoulder by a warm fire."

"Through our very attrition we deny God."

Peter was the undisputed leader of this Christian band of followers. Jesus would at one time say of Peter, *"Upon this rock I will build my church."* Jesus undoubtedly associated with Peter, but when it came to proclaiming Christ in the midst of the enemy's campfire, Peter gave Jesus a cold shoulder. Have you ever been there? God knows I have.

It must appear to the casual observer that Jesus *lives in a box, in a church, that has a locked door that we can only open on Sundays.* That's the only time most people proclaim Him anyway! We sure are "Christian" on Sunday, ain't we? Foot stompin'. Toe tappin', Double clappin' – screamin' Jesus like we actually know Him. Then the worst thing, at least in my estimation happens – service ends. It's almost like we wear the love of God like a coat that we drop off at the church door, only to pick up again in another seven days. Monday through Saturday, we go right back to the fuss and cuss of the world. Through our very attrition we deny God.

Most of us don't actually have the heart to deny Jesus with our mouths, but we do deny Him in our affiliation. Simply put, our choice in company hinders our relationship with God. Peter's first problem wasn't the denial; it was his choice in company. Peter warmed his hands at the enemy's fire – *Hello!* The ENEMY's fire? He not only sought the comfort of the fire, but he also sought the comfort and ease that came with denying Christ – no difficult questions to answer, no persecution to endure, and most importantly, no risk. Peter warmed his hands but froze his heart toward Jesus.

> **Challenge Questions**
>
> *1. What "warm fires" have I given Jesus a "cold shoulder" at? Friendships? Companionships? Convenience? Acceptance? Laziness? Popularity?*
>
> ---
>
> *2. Does my affiliation change my conversation? Do I deny Christ in order to be accepted by the world?*
>
> ---
>
> *3. What did Jesus do when He found out that Peter denied Him? Jesus died for Him, anyway! Jesus could never do to us what we do to Him.*
> *to get off the "bottle"?*

My brother, my sister, the question is – where are the "warm fires" in your life where you've given Jesus the "cold shoulder"? Where are the places and who are the people that have made you forsake your relationship with Jesus? Is your "warm fire" your social circle or your romantic partner? Is your "warm fire" your occupation? Is your "warm fire" your family? Are you your own "warm fire"? Is it your attitude, arrogance, or inflated sense of self-worth? Only you know, but know that warm hands mean a cold heart.

Will you let Jesus in out of the cold today?

Memory Verse: *Also I say unto you, Whosoever shall confess me before men, him shall the Son of man also confess before the angels of God – Luke 12:8*

MODERN DAY

PROVERBS

29

Joy: The AFTER Party

Some people see the glass as half full, while others see it as half empty. Me, I'm just happy to have a cup!

Joy: The AFTER Party

4 A time to weep, and a time to laugh; a time to mourn, and a time to dance;

Ecclesiastes 3:4

5 For his anger lasts only a moment,
but his favor lasts a lifetime!
Weeping may last through the night,
but joy comes with the morning.

Psalm 30:5

Some people see the world as a glass half full, while others see it as a glass half empty; me, I'm just happy to have a cup! Life is about perspective. Perspective determines attitude and attitude determines conduct. Negative people behave negatively because they first thought negatively. Depressed people behave sullenly because they first thought depressed thoughts. Life is not about how it looks at you, but rather how you look at it. Whether life is half full or half empty, you'd better be happy just to have a cup! I'd like to talk to you from the subject, "Joy: The AFTER

Party."

In our two text messages above, I discovered twin revelations. It wasn't the context necessarily that spoke to me but the syntax. I notice that in both texts that the joyous moments came AFTER the sorrowful moments. *Interesting.*

In our first text, Solomon sets forth the Christian calendar with the month of mourning preceding the month of dancing. *Interesting.* The second text declares that "Weeping may last through the night" but after that "joy comes with the morning." Again, interesting!

"God has not promised us immunity from the ills of life.

Family, life happens. Family members die, loved ones leave, jobs and relationships end, we get disappointed, we get denied – life happens! God has not promised us immunity from the ills of life. What, then, is the responsibility placed on the child of God when faced with adversity? Are we not to cry, weep, or feel? God forbid! We hurt like everyone else does. We, too, get knocked down by the TKO's of life. The difference though is that we don't stay that way! It is the true child of God that can stand in the dark shadow of sadness and see through to the glorious light of joy.

Consider our passages. Solomon placed laughing AFTER weeping and dancing AFTER mourning. David placed lifetime AFTER a moment, morning AFTER night, and joy AFTER weeping! God wants you to know that there is an AFTER party! AFTER disappointment there is dancing. AFTER the termination there is triumph. AFTER death there is life. God wants to invite you to the AFTER party of joy, and the price of admission is your faith in God.

The key word to remember is "perspective." How do you see the glass? Half full, half empty, or are you just grateful to have a cup? The reason I praise God for the glass is because as long as I have a glass, He can always empty it if it's too full or fill if it's empty!

Challenge Questions

1. If my attitude was the key that opens the door to my joy, would I be locked out?

---

2. Do situations in my life affect me or do I affect them?

---

3. How can I allow God to change my outlook, so I can change my outcome?

Memory Verse: *So you have sorrow now, but I will see you again; then you will rejoice, and no one can rob you of that joy. – John 16:22*

MODERN DAY

PROVERBS

30

The Bible is Only the Beginning

The Bible is more than God's credit history; it's His promissory note.

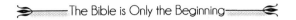

The Bible is Only the Beginning

30 The disciples saw Jesus do many other miraculous signs in addition to the ones recorded in this book.

31 But these are written so that you may continue to believe that Jesus is the Messiah, the Son of God, and that by believing in him you will have life by the power of his name.

John 20:30-31

The Bible is God's Word. It is His divinely inspired assembly of scripture, purposed together on pages, subdivided into 66 books, and distributed over two testaments. The Bible tells us God's history with humanity and our hope for the future, but is the Bible all there is? Is God's dominion, power, glory, and work limited to the papyrus prison of the Holy Book? God forbid. There is so much more to come! "The Bible is Only the Beginning!"

Our Good News springs from the journey of John through 20 chapters with Jesus. John's Gospel offers the most comprehensive record of the life of Jesus Christ. The other three Evangelists – Matthew, Mark, and Luke only capture pieces of Jesus' journey, and their Gospel accounts are referred to as "synoptic"—meaning "a general view of a whole." The

Synoptic Gospels are like snapshots taken of Jesus from a certain distance – useful, but at best, hazy snapshots from the crowd.

> ⇒----)(----⇐
> *"Know that even when you've read the entire Bible from cover to cover, Genesis to Revelation, you've only scooped a cup of water out of God's ocean of knowledge."*
> ⇒----)(----⇐

John jots the most detailed description of the life and times of Jesus Christ, yet when he arrives at the 30th verse of the 20 chapter, he concludes that there is STILL MORE to the story! John says, *"The disciples saw Jesus do many other miraculous signs in addition to the ones recorded in this book."* What? You mean there is MORE?! God spent 39 chapters of the Old Testament telling us of a world He created with his bare hands, a world that hated him, a world He tried to save, and a Savior He promised to send. He then devoted 27 books to the New Testament to make His Word flesh, lived, died, resurrected, sent us His Spirit, founded His church, and then prepared His people for His return. And there's STILL MORE? Family, the Bible is only the beginning!

Know that even when you've read the entire Bible from cover to cover, Genesis to Revelation, you've only scooped a cup of water out of God's ocean of knowledge. The Apostle Paul tells us in 1 Corinthians 13:12 that *"For now we see through a glass, darkly; but then face to face."*

By this Paul meant that even with the knowledge we do have, we don't have nearly as much as we will when we see Jesus face to face for ourselves. Even endowed with the Book of the Bible, we only loosely know the God of the Bible. Far too many of us worship the Book and not the Author of it. The Bible is merely an introduction to the God described in it. Trust me - the Bible is only the beginning!

So what is the Bible good for then?! So glad you asked:

Challenge Questions

1. Do I limit God to the pages of the Bible?

---

2. What miracles do I want God to perform in my life that were not recorded in the Bible?

---

3. Do I trust God to do today what He did over 2,000 years ago?

➤ *To Further Your Faith – "these are written so that you may continue to believe."* The key word in this text is "continue." The Bible doesn't give you faith; God does. The Bible doesn't establish your faith; it furthers it. You either have faith or you don't, but don't expect "faith dust" to fly open from the pages. Most of us though, already have a general faith in God or a sense of Him, however small, so when the Word of God is applied to it, it waters it much like a seed. Reading the Word of God will fertilize your faith.

➢ *To Recognize Real* – *"to believe that Jesus is the Messiah, the Son of God".* If there is one thing that you must leave the Bible knowing is that Jesus IS the Son of God and the Savior of the World! Your salvation doesn't lie in how many Sunday School lessons you've learned or how much "Word" you know – it lies in the profession of your faith. Jesus posed this question to His disciples, "Who do you say that I am?" The purpose of the pages is to prepare you to answer the question with conviction – Jesus is the Messiah, the Son of God. You can meet the prophets when you get to heaven, but Jesus is the Doorman you want to know first!

➢ *To Be Saved* – *"that by believing in him you will have life by the power of his name."* Paul proposes this problem in Romans 10:13 "Whosoever calls on the name of the Lord shall be saved. But how can he believe in whom he has not heard?" The purpose of the Word of God is ultimately to connect the dots of sin to salvation. Faith in God is nice, but salvation of God is supreme. A great many people know who Jesus is, but do not believe in what He does. Remember that the Bible is not a book to be committed to our memory; it tells us of a God who committed His memory to us. After you've read the Word of Truth, you should be moved to act on the Truth. The Bible is like having God's telephone number; once you get it, you should give Him a call!

My brothers and sisters, too many of us have elevated the Bible to a "god" and reduced God to a book. Read the Word but worship God. Our God sits on a throne, not on a shelf. Please part the pages of Truth, as it houses our history and hope with God through Christ Jesus. Just remember that His Story is not history. The Bible is only the beginning! The writers of the book have died, but the God of the book still lives!

Do you know why I'm glad that not ALL of Jesus' miracles were recorded in the Bible? Because it didn't include mine! Are you looking forward to yours? The Bible is Only the Beginning! Stick around to see what He does next!

Memory Verse: *Heaven and earth shall pass away: but my words shall not pass away. – Mark 13:31*

I t's better to be standing on the porch too early, than to be running out of the house too late.

Coming Soon!

7 "Look, I am coming soon! Blessed are those who obey the words of prophecy written in this book"

12 "Look, I am coming soon, bringing my reward with me to repay all people according to their deeds.

13 I am the Alpha and the Omega, the First and the Last, the Beginning and the End."

14 Blessed are those who wash their robes. They will be permitted to enter through the gates of the city and eat the fruit from the tree of life.

20 He who is the faithful witness to all these things says, "Yes, I am coming soon!" Amen! Come, Lord Jesus!

Revelations 22: 7, 12-14, 20

Coming soon to a sinner near you – *Judgment*! While the release date hasn't been published it certainly has been promised – Jesus is coming back soon. Yes – Jesus – the Lamb of God, the Prince of Peace, the Wonderful Counselor – is coming back SOON. *Pastors and priests* have hailed Him as "Savior of the World", *Disciples and followers* proclaim Jesus as a "must see," while *Atheists and nihilists* have "critically acclaimed" Him. Family, I just wanted to wind the film reel and tell you that Jesus

Christ is Coming Soon! Are you ready?

Our final text finds John the Revelator, a sequestered saint on the island of Patmos, penning our Lord's farewell address. The 22nd chapter is the final chapter of the Bible and these few verses conclude our Lord's written discourse with humanity. What I find so intriguing here is the way Jesus begins to end His instruction manual. Through John the Lord declares three times, *"I am coming soon!"* Hey, I'm no smarter than a 5th grader but I know that if God states the same phrase three times within the same chapter of Scripture, that He must be emphasizing a point He wants us to get. In this passage our Lord says, *"I am coming soon!"* Jesus is emphatically certain that He will return to Earth to judge the living and the dead; the question becomes, will you be ready for your court date? *"I am coming soon!"*

> *"...He's not looking for your reflections, He's looking for His reflection. Will your "religion" find you ready?"*

The news that Jesus Christ is "coming soon" could be Good News or Bad News depending on which "subscription" you currently receive. For those in Christ, it is exceedingly Good News that our Lord is returning to open the Life Gate that all who believe may go in. For the believer, Christ's return ends a death sentence to the ephemeral existence of our earthen bodies. Simply put, for a child of God – Christ's return is gonna be ALL THAT! On the other hand, for those not YET in Christ, the "return" of this "Jesus" is

unsettling at the very least. There are those who have refused to believe, clinging to intellect and beholding to a belief system that doesn't require salvation. There are some still who have nullified the need for "religion," relegating themselves to a life of self-reliance and self-righteous theology. What I can tell you about a "me-phi-me" religion is that Christ's Judgment will not be in essay format! On that day, He's not looking for your reflections; He's looking for His reflection. Will your "religion" find you ready?

Finally, there are those (perhaps you), who have not yet accepted Christ because they simply have not been offered the opportunity. If that is you, then I consider it sheer joy to tell you the Good News of Jesus Christ. Our God loved us so much that in spite of our sinful nature, myriad of mistakes, and exceeding evil, He ordered His only Begotten Son to bear the fate that was rightly due our name. At Calvary, Jesus Christ carried the sins of the world upon His back in the form of an old, rugged, splintered wooden cross. For our sake, He endured the abandonment of friends and family, the public shame of mockery, and ultimately the vile cruelty of death by crucifixion. The price our sin demanded – the price our Savior paid. And what does Jesus want in return?

It's simple family – He wants us to be ready when He comes back!

In this passage, Jesus gives us 3 practical points of preparation:

➢ *Obey His Word – "Blessed are those who obey the words of prophecy written in this book."* There is no way to arrive at an appointed destination without directions, in that way, there is NO WAY to get to God's Divine Destination in right knowledge without knowing and obeying His Word.

Notice that while knowledge is important, God emphasized obedience; knowing the Word is one thing – obeying the Word is another. God not only wants you to know what the Bible says, He wants you to *do* what the Bible says. Knowing the speed limit and obeying the speed limit are two different things.

> *Clean Up Your Life – "Blessed are those who wash their robes. They will be permitted to enter through the gates of the city and eat the fruit from the tree of life."* In restaurants you'll notice a sign on the mirrors in most bathrooms that reads, "All Employees Must Wash Hands Before Returning." That's what preparing for Christ's return is like. You wouldn't serve a houseguest a meal you plucked out of the garbage, would you? The same is with our personal preparation for

> **Challenge Questions**
>
> *1. Where do I want to be found when Christ returns: standing on the porch or running out of the house?*
>
> ---
>
> *2. If I died today, where would I spend eternity?*
>
> ---
>
> *3. Jesus is coming back to Earth to go back to Heaven. Will I go with Him?*

~224~

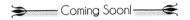 Coming Soon!

Christ – You must wash your hands!

> *Be Ready and Be Excited - He who is the faithful witness to all these things says, "Yes, I am coming soon!" Amen! Come, Lord Jesus!* John gets so happy penning this passage that He taps his shoutin' shoes and exclaims, "Amen! Come, Lord Jesus!" This, too, should be our attitude when facing the Judgment. For the believer, Judgment is a homecoming celebration; there is no need for fear when you have faith.

In the end, the only question that matters is, where will YOU stand in the courtroom of Christ's return? When your case comes before the Judge, will you have reliable representation? At this very moment, are you certain that your lawyer would even show up? If you're finding it difficult to answer these questions, might I inform you that God ensured your inalienable right to "free representation" and that Jesus Christ will take your case? He's only one "call" away.

Jesus Christ IS coming soon. Salvation + Preparation = Acceptance.

Memory Verse: *Be ye therefore ready also: for the Son of man cometh at an hour when ye think not. – Luke 12:40*

Afterword

This is just the beginning. God's word is full of gems that can adorn your life with the peace, love, and joy that we all seek. His word is a compass to every traveler, irrespective of the path he is on. If you are seeking forgiveness from the past and looking for a new start, this is the way. If you already are walking with Him and just need a course correction, this is the way. If you are leading others or raising a family, this is the way. Regardless of where you're coming from, God's word is the path to where you're going. Christ said it best, "I am the way the truth and the life. No man comes to the father except through me."

If you are ready to admit that you're lost, God is ready to step in through Jesus Christ and lead you home. Home is a place where He is your father, and you are his child and all he has is yours. That means your peace, your joy, your future, your power, your freedom, all the goodies in Daddy's house belong to you. And no good thing will he withold from those he loves.

Maybe you're saying, "That sounds nice, really it does. But you don't know where I've been and what I've done. There's no way God wants to hear from me now." There is nothing you can do to extinguish the fire of God's love for you and His love is never in question. "God demonstrated his love for us in this, while we were YET sinners, Christ died for us." He didn't wait until we got it together, or we were wise enough to make a request. He made the first move. He reached out, knowing everything about us, and knowing what we would do even before we did it, and he died ANYWAY. Knowing that one day you would be in this place at this time, in need of his grace, he did it anyway. So His love is not in question.

Maybe you're saying, "I appreciate the wise words, and I'll apply them, but religion is not for me. I can do this on my own." But you can't. No one can. And if religion is not for you, join the club, because Christ is not about creating a new set of laws and rules to confine and confuse you.

He is about mending a broken relationship between you and your Creator who is waiting to embrace and fulfill you in ways that money, sex, drugs, friends, family, and fame cannot, and if we're honest, have not. Religion is not what he is offering. He is more than a way of life. He is life itself. And apart from him, his words cannot be applied. They require more than human effort and good will because "all have sinned and fallen short of the glory of God." With this in mind, he offered himself as the Holy Spirit to come and counsel us and help us apply his word, because he knew we would have trouble doing it on our own. This isn't about how good you can be, but how good He can be if you let Him in.

If you are tired of traveling in circles and are ready to move on towards your destination of peace, joy, love, fulfillment, and abundance in life that Christ died to give you, if you are tired of being consumed by the flames of worry, doubt, anxiety, depression and despair, then recall our grade-school mantra: **STOP DROP and ROLL.**

STOP trying to direct your life without the help of the life-giver. Halt all attempts at correcting yourself that do not include Him.

 Afterword

Drop the façade. He already knows you fully and loves you still. Admit you are lost.

Roll on out of the driver seat, and let Jesus take the wheel (thanks Carrie J).

-*Minister Gabrielle Pierre*

If you're ready say this prayer out loud:

Jesus, I've really messed up. I've done wrong, and walked far away from you and far away from home. Trying to run my own life has not gotten me far and now I'm lost. I believe you lived on this earth to show me the way and you died on the cross to pay the price for my journey home. I believe you're alive and I want you to live in my heart. I receive you as a gift I could never earn, and offer you my heart as a throne. Jesus, please receive me and lead me from this day on. I'm ready to come home.

If you prayed this prayer, you have become a child of God. This gift has yet to be unwrapped. Find a church home where you can grow with people who are willing and open to receive you and all of your questions, because you will have them. If you need help doing so, or to share your story of self discovery contact us at:

gpi@godzchildproductions.net

Acknowledgements

I have planted, Apollos watered; but God gave the increase. – 1 Corinthians 3:6(KJV)

What is it for man to claim credit when God gets the glory? The Lord God Himself wrote, edited, and published this book. What an awesome vision He poured into the hearts and hands of the team it took to produce this literary offering. This book literally required a village to raise it. I never started this journey with the intentions of writing a book. I began to post daily devotionals and status messages onto Facebook, and one day Shaun Saunders(my good friend and now publisher), made the prophetic observation, "these messages are like Modern Day Proverbs". From that day forward we knew that the Lord was up to something. What a mighty God we serve!

To My Lord & Savior

Praise ye the LORD. O give thanks unto the LORD; for he is good: for his mercy endureth for ever – Psalm 106:1

For forgiving my sins, saving my soul, and giving me life more abundantly – Thank YOU! Lord I pray that Your will be done through this book. Forgive me - I'm far less than You have asked me. I love You – you have been far more than I've asked you to be. Please accept this book as the first of many attempts to repay your love.

 Acknowledgments

To My Wife, Monique

"At last!" the man exclaimed.
"This one is bone from my bone,
and flesh from my flesh!
She will be called 'woman,'
because she was taken from 'man.'" – Genesis 2:23(NLT)

I praise the Lord for every breath you take. You are my heart's guard. Surely, I have found favor in the sight of the Lord because He has entrusted a treasure like you into my care. You are the focus for my fire and the practicality for my idealism. I not only love you, I need you. I am grateful for your silent sacrifices and outspoken support. I pray that grace grants us many more years and books together.

To My Daughter Jaylynn

Children are a gift from the Lord; they are a reward from him. – Psalm 127:3(NLT)

I have always been proud of you; I pray that I have made you proud of me. I love you. I live for you. I'd gladly die for you. You're old enough to read and understand this book, so get ready to do both. I look forward to discussing the chapters with you.

To My Mom & Dad

"Honor your father and mother. Then you will live a long, full life in the land

the Lord your God is giving you. – Exodus 20:12

You not only gave me life; you gave me love. You came to my football games before I played well, supported my preaching before I preached well, and praised my book before you even read it. Your unyielding love is my secret to success. You have taught me the value of hard work and the importance of humility. Your baby boy is an author!

To My Publisher, Editor, and Brother – Shaun Saunders
I thank my God upon every remembrance of you, - Philippians 1:3(KJV)

Not only are you God's child, you are God's friend. You have a heart after God and a mind to match. The only attribute that outpaces your talent is your humility. You have been my friend during my friendless days, my encouragement during my down days, and now my usher into the literary ministry. Not only do you believe in God; you believe in me. How do I say thank you for that? I pray that I make you proud.

To "Mrs.Everything" – Ana Saunders
I don't say this because I want a gift from you. Rather, I want you to receive a reward for your kindness. – Philippians 4:17(NLT)

I would disrespect your sacrifice to list you by one title; you are Mrs.Everything. Most great men have a great women behind them; Shaun is blessed to have you beside him. You are a shining example of Christian

womanhood and loving devotion. There's no Shaun without you and if that's the case, then there's no Modern Day Proverbs without you either. We thank and love you for your support.

The Woman Behind the Art – Patricia Tibere

This is why I remind you to fan into flames the spiritual gift God gave you when I laid my hands on you. – 2 Timothy 1:6(NLT)

From the first day I met you and heard of your gift, I told you that the Lord was looking for someone with "more faith than talent" for this book. You abound in both faith and talent, and I praise our Lord that Modern Day Proverbs has served as your anointed art exhibit. Your hand prints are all over this book – from the front to back covers, and every page in between. I pray that the Lord has demonstrated his Divine intent to you; you are His illustrator. Stay on the path; you haven't seen anything yet!

To My Publication Partners

And we know that all things work together for good to them that love God, to them who are the called according to his purpose. – Romans 8:28(KJV)

You have no idea how much I needed you. I had the ministry but none of the money. At the start of this project I was fearful that this great vision would have to be aborted but I was reminded that where God gives vision He also makes provision. He worked on your hearts to put this book in the world's hands. You all truly made this possible. I have received support from close friends and perfect strangers. I have been blessed by family I talk to every day and some I've never met. For all you've done – I love you and thank you!

With no "respect of persons" (Acts 10:34), here are my Publication Partners:

Olivia Withers, Myron Covington, Sandra Johnson, Debra Alexis, Laudaine Simeon, Marlisa Spruill, Kim Harrison, Dreamela Furgerson-Neal, Myra Moore, Rick Briamonte, Naja Thomas, Chasity Richardon, Lawrence and Deloise Alexander, Yvette Alexander, Rev.Keisha Harris, Lyvonne Briggs, Richard Hill, Christina King, Brandi Nicole Warren, Rev.Frederick Hanna, Jeff Anthony, Michael and Kathleen Morrison, Lowell Harwood, Sandra and Richard Alexander, Eric Currence, Christina McSwain, Deacon Reggie Shivers, Charles and Malika Herring, Linda Raoul, Nisheena Smith, Dominique Cruz-Tucker, Catricia Shaw, April Morgan, Nick Edwards, and Antonio Forcelles.